SEE THE UNSEEN

STEP INTO A DEEP RELATIONSHIP WITH GOD AND LIVE FROM YOUR TRUE IDENTITY

MASON KUHR

This book goes out to my Lord and Savior, Jesus Christ, the risen Messiah and King of all. Thank you for never giving up on me while filling the void in my life of a true brother and guiding me even when I didn't know who you were.

This is a testament to your ability to transform and guide us into a reborn life.

HERE'S A GIFT BEFORE YOU BEGIN

Visit https://whop.com/lionheart/ to get access to Lionheart
Project: a ninety-day leadership transformation program, faith-led
builder & creator community, and holistic reset protocol.

TABLE OF CONTENTS

INTRODUCTION

Imagine this:

You're lying in bed at 10:00 p.m., if you're lucky, scrolling through another person's content, wondering if this will finally be the answer to the nagging pit in your gut that never seems to be satisfied. There's an emptiness that comes with performing for a grace that's already been given to you by God, but still thinking you have to earn it, or not even realizing it. All you want is the peace of knowing that you're exactly where you need to be, with the clarity to understand who is taking you where you're going.

Tomorrow you'll wake up and try again—the meditation app, the prayer routine, the latest bio-hack that promises complete clarity in all areas of your life. You may resort to pushing through another day of success and striving that feels hollow, relationships that feel surface level compared to where you want them to be, and a gnawing sense that you're missing something essential, while operating out of alignment with your true design.

You know God is real, but you're still not 100 percent sold, if you're being honest. You can feel it to be true, or at least you think and hope that you do, and you believe it. But how deeply do you believe? Do you still have some unbelief? Do you encounter him? Believing is one thing; knowing and *experiencing* are two whole different things, and the gap between them is killing you.

Maybe you've tried church, or go consistently, and left feeling like you got an emotional high but no true change. Maybe you go out of obligation, neglecting the fact that you're first meant to be the church that God dwells in. Maybe you've explored other paths— meditation retreats, plant medicine, wellness protocols—gathering small pieces of truth but never finding the whole. Maybe you read the Bible consistently and push yourself to be a "good Christian," yet you find yourself striving for love without the heart for it. Maybe you're successful by every external measure, yet internally you're fragmented, searching for something you can't quite name.

The Problem Nobody Talks About

Here's what's really happening: You're spiritually nearsighted. Not blind—you can see shapes and shadows of truth. You catch glimpses of God moving in your life. But everything is blurry, undefined, like looking through fogged glasses you can't seem to clean.

This isn't your fault. We live in a world that teaches us to see everything except what matters most, and our past can distort our beliefs. We're trained from childhood to focus on the visible—achievements, appearances, acquisitions—while the invisible realm where God actually moves remains hidden from view.

He is Spirit, after all!

The result? You end up with a life that looks good but feels dull. You chase spiritual experiences and emotional highs like merit badges, hoping the next one will finally make you whole. You perform for

God the same way you perform for the world, never realizing he doesn't want your performance—he wants your presence. He wants you.

What You're Actually Searching For

That restlessness you feel? It's not random. It's your soul recognizing that it was made for more than surface-level existence. What you're really seeking isn't another spiritual technique or religious formula. You're seeking a direct, undeniable, transformative encounter with the living God.

You want to:

- See yourself the way God sees you—not through the lens of your failures or successes, but through his eyes of perfect love.
- Experience his presence as a living reality, not just a concept you intellectually accept.
- Break free from the exhausting cycle of spiritual searching and finally feel at home in your own soul, with certainty of who God actually is.
- Live with the kind of grounded confidence that comes from knowing who you are and whose you are.
- Move through the world with spiritual sight, seeing the eternal significance in everyday moments.
- Develop your discernment and wisdom to deeper levels.

Why Most Approaches Fall Short

The problem with most spiritual teaching—whether from the pulpit or the podcast—is that it gives you more to *do* without addressing who you're *being*. It adds another practice to your already overwhelming routine without dealing with the fundamental issue: You're trying to see spiritual reality through natural eyes, and a confused mind, instead of spiritual identity.

It's like trying to see the stars through a microscope. The tool isn't broken; you're just using it wrong.

Religious legalities often make this worse by turning grace-led relationship into performance. Most give you rules to follow and boxes to check, but they can't give you the one thing your soul is actually craving: genuine, intimate, transformative connection with your Creator.

Do you have to have rules to sit in the presence of your Dad? No. But if you do, that can also be a reason you're here.

Meanwhile, the spiritual-but-not-religious path leaves you drowning in options. It can deliver healing, but it's a hamster wheel that never resolves. I have gone down too many holistic healing paths to count, from meditation to somatic healing work, fascia work, herbal healing, energetic nutrition, detox and nervous system recalibration, and so much more to know that although they help heal, the core *dis-ease* is in our identity. Every teacher has a different map, and every practice promises breakthrough, but without a true North Star and recognition of who God actually is, and who you are in relation, you just end up walking in circles, accumulating experiences but never arriving anywhere.

The Promise of This Book

This book isn't another spiritual technique to add to your collection. It's not about doing more—it's about seeing differently. When you learn to see through God's eyes instead of your own limited perspective, everything changes.

In these pages, you'll discover:

- Why your past (especially your relationship with your parents) has created a lens that distorts how you see God, and how to clean that lens
- How to recognize the difference between hypervigilance (trauma response) and true spiritual discernment

- The hidden agreements you've made that keep you spiritually stuck, and how to break them
- Why surrender isn't weakness but the ultimate power move that unlocks supernatural sight
- How to transform your sensitivity from a burden into a spiritual superpower
- Practical protocols for maintaining spiritual clarity in a world designed to fog your vision

But more than techniques, you'll discover what it means to stop seeking God's gifts and start seeking God himself. Because when you find him—really find him, not just know about him—you'll realize you've found everything you've been searching for.

Your Journey Starts Here

I know you're tired. Tired of searching, tired of trying, tired of feeling like you're one revelation away from breakthrough but it never quite arrives. I know because I lived it, which you'll learn more about in the next few pages. But I also know there's a way through—not around, not over, but through.

This journey will require you to face things you've been avoiding. It will ask you to feel emotions you've spent years suppressing. It will challenge every false agreement you've made about who you are and how love works.

But on the other side of that discomfort is the life you've been searching for: whole, aligned, deeply rooted in a love that will never leave you empty.

You don't have to keep running on the spiritual hamster wheel, exhausting yourself with endless seeking. The truth you're looking for isn't out there somewhere—it's waiting to meet you here, in the mess and beauty of your actual life.

If you're ready to stop searching in circles and start seeing clearly, if you're willing to let go of who you think you are to discover who God says you are, then welcome. You're exactly where you need to be.

The journey from spiritual blindness to sight isn't easy, but it's real. And it starts with one simple recognition:

You were made to see the unseen. And with God's help, you will.

Let's begin.

HOW THIS BOOK HAPPENED

About six years ago, around the Covid era, I heard God's voice for the first time. It wasn't a guess that it was him; it *was* him. When you hear that voice, you can't go back.

I remember that I was sitting in my bed after feeling extremely lost and going through a depressing time period in my life. I had lost my identity as an athlete, lost a relationship, lost friends, lost everything I thought I was. It was the first time I encountered the void of noth-ingness . . . and I *did not* want to be there.

I spent my time drinking a handle of liquor each weekend to cope with the never-ending thoughts that I didn't want to face, embrac-ing the life of a college-kid.

I listened to music, like King Saul in the Old Testament, to keep myself from feeling tormented. And I distracted myself by spend-ing multiple nights out of the week by going up to my local college campus bars and using scripted pickup lines to get some sort of validation from women, confirming that I was still a man inside.

I was scared and confused, but I didn't want to admit it.

Now if you told me then that I would be seeking a deeper relationship with Jesus every day, I wouldn't have believed it for a second and would've told you to kick rocks. I didn't need no man telling me what to do!

It took me a long time to get to the point that I would actually sit in silence and observe what was going on in my mind. Because every time I got close, I would feel a wave of panic that felt like dying. And it was dying. I was dying to myself. It required me to feel all the things I didn't want to feel.

I went down a spiritual rabbit hole looking for meaning, discovering books like *The Secret* and *The Power of Now* to start to feel like I had some control of reality. And honestly, at the time, I thought that they were great and what I needed in my spiritual infancy. I learned how to expand my awareness and observe my thought patterns, making a conscious effort every single day walking to my college classes while purposefully looking in front of me as well as out of my peripheral vision so that I could take in more of the world through wider sight. I would ask myself why I was doing what I was doing as I was doing it, to be very intentional of each moment. I'd start to catch negative thought patterns and tell myself the opposite. I was rewiring my brain in real time.

As great as all of this was, though, there was still something missing. A purpose. A mission. My masculine soul was crying out for meaning and a reason to be alive.

I don't remember the exact date, but I do remember that one night, I was sitting in my bed and meditating on what my purpose in life was. I kept asking the question over and over, like transcendental meditation, hoping that eventually, when the meaning of the words faded out, the meaning of life would fade in.

As I went deeper and deeper, to the point I was almost asleep, I heard something said to me that would change my life forever: *"See the unseen."*

It didn't just sound like a human voice. It was a voice of power. It was the equivalent of getting hit by a train and smacking the ground while skydiving with no parachute at the same time. I launched up out of my bed, staring at the wall, trying to comprehend what I had just heard. I knew it was God. There was no doubt.

Since then, that phrase has come up over and over in my life, and it still does. It was in YouTube videos that "randomly" popped up, although nothing is a coincidence. It was in other books I read. I would hear it said in a casual conversation. It was just weird … but it did affirm to me that I needed to understand what it meant.

Well, after following that phrase to infinity and beyond, I ended up moving out of Ohio to Florida on a two-month notice. I had my supplement brand, the Stampede Network, grow so rapidly that it probably contributed to me losing my hair. I ended up on some crazy plant medicine journeys. (I am not telling you to do this, nor do I condone it. I do not do this anymore, but I have made a commitment to write this book from authentic life experience as much as I can recall. It's been so much that I have to say, "As I can recall.")

I climbed to the top of Mount Kilimanjaro. I traveled to more than ten countries in a little over a year and lived out a big chunk of my bucket list at this point.

I have had one of the deepest and most eye-opening relationships I've ever experienced in my life that has helped me know the love of Jesus. I've released more lies and blocks in myself than I can comprehend, while always on the journey to uncover more.

It has been so eventful, but it's also been a blur. Partly because I was striving, and partly because I was flowing in that striving.

It took me a long time to uncover the meaning of "See the unseen," but since I've seen it, I can't go back. And you know, even as I think

I know the meaning now, God may still give it deeper revelation in the future. That's one of the things I've noticed that he does a lot, so don't try to put him in a box and say you've figured it all out. As it says in Proverbs 20:24 (NLT), "The Lord directs our steps, so why try to understand everything along the way?"

So as we get into this book, I want to preface it with this. I'm not trying to be some eloquent writer. I'm very direct, and I like to keep it raw. Some sections may be highly organized, and there may be some that are very action focused. It will flow how it comes out naturally as I write it.

My goal for you by the end of this is to know that a spiritual reality is not only possible, but also very normal. I want you to be able to see through a lens that is guided by your Creator so that you can live in more alignment and purpose, while being able to handle the ups and downs of life more effectively.

When you have an eternal perspective, life takes a whole new meaning. Instead of being stuck on the ground, you can gain the eyes of an eagle flying above. Maintain this connection, and there will be a lot more harmony and adventure in your life.

You most likely have a lot of blocks in your mind based on your beliefs and upbringing, emotionally and mentally. I'm not excluded, and life is a journey of releasing them, so I don't pretend I'm perfect. These keep you from seeing not only others correctly, but also yourself and God. We will address those within this book, because that is one of the biggest driving forces—if not the biggest—of what keeps you stuck and disconnected. Pride can keep us from willingly choosing to see what's true and what isn't, which is usually where God intervenes.

I write all of this from personal experience, from knowledge and wisdom acquired, and from the ongoing relationship I've built with Jesus, whom I recognize as God, and who came to live among us (and is still doing so).

Many of the words in here have been collected over a period of about five deeply challenging yet rewarding years. My life has been one giant unveiling process, seeking the truth above all, only to discover that the truth was relative to my identity at the time, not the truth by God's definition. But now that I've discovered who the truth really is: a Man born in Nazareth, I now have the ability to share from a deeper, more grounded understanding.

I am not here to preach to you. I'm an embodiment of the journey itself. I am by no means perfect, but I'm a man who desires to grow, learn, and love the truth more and more each day.

If I could sum up why this is such an important book to read on your faith journey, here it is: *If the enemy can cloud your vision, he can pull you away from your spiritual mission.*

I wrote this book not just as a way to unlock a new perspective, but also to use it for going to war. This is a transformational guidebook. Each chapter is followed by an implementation activity list to be used each week. Don't just read; make sure to implement.

I love to engage with those who enjoy my work and are impacted by it, so feel free to reach out to @masonkuhr on all socials if you have any questions or want to continue your spiritual development and self-mastery journey. I'm excited for what your future holds as you start to see things in a new way.

Introduction Implementation: Week 1

Each chapter will have an implementation focus for a week. Do *not* continue to the next chapter until you implement the steps from the previous one, and if it's a recurring action, come back to the next chapter in one week.

Teaching Point

You're not broken for feeling lost—that void you're trying to fill with endless searching is actually God calling you home. The same voice that said, "See the unseen" to me in my darkness is waiting to transform your restless seeking into grounded purpose.

Mindset Shift

From "I need to find the answer out there" to "The answer has been pursuing me all along."

Prayer

"Lord, I want to see the unseen. Help me push through the panic of silence to find you waiting there. Give me the courage to die to my false self so that my true self in you can live. Open my eyes to see life through your lens, not mine. Thank you for directing my steps, even when I don't understand the path. In Jesus's name, amen."

Scriptures to Meditate On

- "The Lord directs our steps, so why try to understand everything along the way?" (Prov. 20:24 NLT).
- "Open my eyes, that I may see wondrous things from Your law" (Ps. 119:18 NKJV).

• "Be still, and know that I am God" (Ps. 46:10 ESV).

Action Steps

1. **Face the silence.** Sit in complete silence for ten minutes per day. When the panic comes, don't run. That's the old you dying. Let it happen; just feel in your body where you are tense and blocked.

2. **Expand your vision.** Take a walk and practice seeing with your peripheral vision while looking straight ahead like I did. Take in more of the world. Notice what you've been missing and how things may feel more present.

3. **Ask the question.** Tonight, before bed, meditate on this question: "What is my purpose?" Don't force an answer. Just keep asking and feel God's prompting. Do this every day for a week; let it be the last thing you ask.

CHAPTER 1 THE CURE TO BLINDNESS

I know exactly where you are.

You want a better relationship with God—not on the surface, but a deeply fulfilling one. People tell you all the time that they're having these amazing relationships with God. And you look around, thinking, "Why is everyone having such a good relationship except me? Why does it feel like, no matter where I look, everyone's talking about hearing God and seeing God and experiencing all these supernatural, amazing things, but I just can't seem to do it?"

Trust me, I've been in the exact same position. I've been like a ping-pong ball bouncing through life, just jumping around trying to find my way but not understanding why I wasn't tapped in with God as much as I wanted to be, why I still felt lost even when I thought I found him.

One of the biggest realizations I had on my journey was this: Even if my mind thought I saw God, my heart did not.

The Split Between Head and Heart

We have to realize that we are spiritual beings having a human experience. And because we have the human-experience part of it, that means we have to get our bodies and ourselves in alignment so we can even hear him in the first place. We have a brain, a heart, and a soul. If only our brain is activated, then we're going to be trying to conceptualize and think about God all the time without feeling him.

But you can't have a relationship with just a thought.

Imagine your dad. If all you did was think, "Hey, this is my dad, this is my dad, this is my dad," you're not actually going to feel connected to him. There are a lot of people who've grown up in that situation. I had an experience like that for a long time: If the heart is not connected, then you feel distant. You know they're your dad, but you don't feel that they're your dad all of the time. You don't feel the actual connection on all levels. All you can do is conceptualize it. You know that they're there, but they're not really a part of your deeper life.

It's not until we activate the heart and start seeing through the eyes of the heart and sync it with the mind that we can see God clearly and have a real relationship with him in the first place (and our fathers as well, but that's a different point).

The Questions Nobody Wants to Ask

To begin seeing clearly, we have to look at the blocks in ourselves that are preventing us from wanting to see clearly. And here are the hard questions you have to ask yourself honestly:

"I say I want to have a relationship with God, but do I actually want to? And have my actions shown that? And if I don't, why not?"

It's not necessarily that you want to have a relationship with God. That can be your ego wanting to have a relationship with him. You have to ask yourself, "Is my soul actually getting access to have a relationship with him? Do I truly want to have a relationship with him at a deeper level?"

So ask yourself: "Do I really want him? Do I want God? Or do I just want what comes with God?"

That's the thing you have to check. Is your desire an actual desire coming from the heart, or is it coming from the mind? You can think that you want something, but under the surface, you feel scared of it. And that's why you end up not having it.

This is the basis of all self-sabotage. We push away what we want, whether from unworthiness, fear in general, or something else. But it's always rooted in fear.

First, you have to check your own heart. Ask yourself if you're truly ready and want to. And if not? That's something to sit and explore. Invite God into that!

Digging Up the Roots

You have to remove those blocks in yourself that keep you from seeing clearly—emotionally, mentally, and physically. The best way I've found to do this is to reconcile your past and dissect all the things that have led up to who you are now. Your traumas. Your relationship with your parents. The people around you. Any of the pains you've gone through.

Two pains that I experienced were that I felt like my dad was distant, and I felt like my mom overly loved me. Whether these things are true or not, they were true for me, so they became parts of my story. This isn't a judgment on them because they were both doing their own thing. They had both gone through their own lessons and experiences and were doing the best they could. I know they love me, and they're amazing parents. But I felt like love was a distant thing that I couldn't get too close to. I couldn't have it with me unless I was performing or striving for it. I had to go out and earn love, and it would run away if I stopped performing.

I believed that even though God's love was always there with me, I couldn't see it. I had a belief from the things that I could see that I wasn't worthy, that I had to shut down my dark emotions. Due to my own self-delusion, I wasn't able to be validated in those things and bring them to light. I was like a circus monkey trying to perform my way to a better existence, and I had no idea that the joy I was seeking was within me, being repressed by false beliefs.

I grew up in an environment that wasn't perfect. There are emotional issues and dysfunctions in every family. But in mine, I felt like I wasn't able to express the anger and frustration I had without negative repercussions, so I didn't bother. I've had to move through that on my own and learn what healthy conflict resolution looks like inside myself. I had to process those things and look at myself so I could understand why they were there in the first place.

The Day Everything Broke

I vividly remember one particular Saturday in college. It was one of those bright, sunny days perfect for a "darty"—those daytime parties on someone's lawn that spiral into messy drunken gatherings. The grass was filled with people barely conscious, laughing at nothing. Stumbling around with drinks in hand. Music blared so loud you could feel it in your chest. The heavy scents of weed and alcohol created this overwhelming, numbing atmosphere. Oh man, how it felt like heaven to my disconnected self! Until it didn't.

I was there because a friend had invited me, but he never even showed. He had probably passed out somewhere before he got there or was trying to pick up some chick while drooling on her shoulder incoherently. I felt completely off balance and anxious, wandering aimlessly through the crowd like I was trapped behind an invisible glass wall. I was observing but not participating. My feet occasionally sticking to the spilled alcohol on the ground as I circled, searching for any familiar face but finding none.

Eventually, the anxiety became too intense, and the weed and dab pen smoke were starting to amplify these long-suppressed feelings. I quietly slipped away, head down, avoiding everyone's gazes as I walked home.

Back in my room, I collapsed onto my bed, completely overwhelmed. All the thoughts I'd been running from for years flooded in. Unworthiness. Grief. Fear. Anxiety. Sadness. Self-hatred. Memories of past rejections, failed relationships, and unmet expectations replayed vividly. I knew I couldn't pretend anymore.

That night, I allowed myself to break. I let the emotions wash over me, raw and unfiltered. Without trying to push them away or numb myself. And somehow in that brokenness, while I lay there dying, something shifted inside me.

I started to feel peace trying to break through.

The Pattern You Can't Unsee

I've had friends who I felt didn't want to be around me. I didn't know why. I thought there was something off about me. I thought I was weird and that being weird was bad. I was also overthinking and not trusting them, out of projection. I'd try to conform with other people, and I would end up just abandoning myself in the process. Trying to fit into other people's lives as the person who didn't want to be a part of the group.

I always felt different in a way, and I didn't understand why kids my age operated the way they did. It felt like most were untrustworthy. When I was younger, I gravitated a lot to those who were struggling in some way on the outside but had pure hearts filled with innocence. Like Jacob in kindergarten, a blind kid in a wheelchair whom I taught to catch a ball.

I made some "friends" who were more acquaintances, but they were like distant friendships, relationships that weren't actually aligned. I also had some really deep one-on-one friendships, but I never really found a tribe or group. I was a free agent. I was so scared of the feeling of being alone because I didn't know that God was there to let me lean on him, so I'd seek out relationships but still isolate myself. Even writing this, I see that there was so much confusion in how to relate with others, I just wanted to keep my distance.

Because of that, I ended up in solitude a lot. But it was not solitude to have a relationship with God; it was solitude out of self-reliance. I was just building a friendship with myself, but God was not fully in the equation from my heart. I secretly resented those around me or was jealous, feeling like I was betrayed or abandoned by them.

But at the same time, I found peace and security in it.

I wanted a deep relationship, and I wanted multiple relationships. But every time I would get close to people, I felt like they would run away. Or they didn't want to be around me. Or my intensity was too much for them. So I had to come to terms with those emotions. My entire life, I've been suppressing them, and I told myself this story out of pride, that I wasn't worth being a friend to or having a relationship with.

I was, of course, part of the problem here. I was in the equation! Have you ever noticed how what you believe about yourself tends to show up in your life?

Because I had that belief, what happened in reality is that I started attracting experiences that reflected those back to me. God made a perfect system: When we believe something, he will allow experiences to reflect that. He allows us to feel the pain, the sadness, the underlying emotions we don't want to feel so that we can move through them and get to a place of purity. He makes an environment around us that is meant to purify us and sanctify us into our actual form. This is the form we're meant to live in—in purity and alignment with him.

Your Relationships Tell the Truth

Here's a little hint that you can use: Your relationships around you are an exact reflection of your relationship with God.

Think about it. If they feel distant? That means God is feeling distant in your life. If you feel like you have to lean on your relationships to receive love? That means you feel like you're not getting love fully from God; they're always showing you what is going on. If you have surface-level relationships and you don't feel any depth to them? That probably means you have a performative relationship with God, lacking depth of intimacy.

I've experienced every single one of these things. So I want you to know as you read this—I have been in your shoes. This has been a struggle in my life I've learned to get to the root of after twenty-six years, thanks to God's grace and mercy, and the ability to feel the pain I need to feel while grieving the feelings hidden inside me.

It's a process of overcoming and undoing. You can go most of your life—and most people do—where you don't even realize these things you're feeling. Many people never even take the chance to look at them. So you have to honestly seek it so deeply that it's the only thing that matters.

Just like the Bible says, "Seek first the kingdom and all these things shall be given to you" (Matt. 6:33, paraphrased). There comes a point in your life where the pain and the wounds and all the things you've been carrying your entire life start to derail everything around you. You don't understand why. And eventually, when they're gone, when they've fallen apart and you have nothing left, the only thing left to lean on is God. And that vacuum is the place where he can help and transform you.

The Cover-Ups We Use

One of the biggest things I dealt with was not pride, but lust. Not just lust of the flesh or sexuality—also lust for food. Lust for acquisition in business. Lusting over things in the world.

Lust is just a cover-up for a lack of intimacy with God, and it's not until we slow down that we can see that. When you slow down, you allow God to speed up your healing.

Remember: It's only in God's presence that we can get to the root of our problems, because he can see them before we ever could. When we don't live in that, we get stuck in sensational living rather than holy relationship.

I didn't feel I had a secure, firm, loving relationship with God that filled me up and allowed me to overflow and give love unconditionally to others. Instead, I felt like I had to receive love by doing things, by going out and trying to get love from outside of me. I couldn't see that it was inside me the whole time.

The tricky thing is that I thought I had a good relationship with God. But when we've grown up in a world where we haven't experienced "great," we'll take "good" and think that's the highest we can get. We don't even know there's something better out there. It doesn't even make sense to us. We can't even conceptualize it from where we're at.

So we stay stuck. We get comfortable at the level of good when we've come from what we think is bad; therefore, we never actually get to great. This is a curse we have to overcome. We have to be willing to explore ourselves and our emotions and our beliefs and everything inside of us.

Your Body Never Lies

Your physical body is always showing you what you believe. If your shoulders are hunched over, you may be carrying a lot of shame. You may be carrying a lot of weight. If you feel overweight at times, usually that can be an indication of feeling unworthy. Even if you've worked out all the time, you try to get weight off your body, but it always comes back. You don't feel like you're worthy of actually maintaining it. There can be deep, shameful wounds inside all of us.

This is what happened in the Garden of Eden when Adam and Eve sinned. They tried to hide after eating the apple. God knew where they were. He gave them an opportunity to come clean, but they still wanted to hide. They don't want to own up to the truth because they thought there was a negative repercussion to it, which there was, but they didn't want to choose love over the feelings of pain and loss.

Let me tell you this as someone who's dealt with deep wounds around these in my life. Shame and guilt? They're way different. Guilt is tied to an action and can help convict you in a way that propels you toward holier living through repentance. Shame is tied to your identity, keeps you stuck in the past, and becomes an invisible god of its own that we use to feel "safe," just like Adam did. Yet it's a cover-up for fear and isolates us from God while pushing us into self-preservation.

The hardest thing to do is face shame, because shame is tied to who you are. And to face shame and move through it, you have to be willing to admit you've been lying to yourself. You have to feel the feeling of dying. You have to let your identity die. That's what it means to die to yourself and renew your mind.

When you keep reaffirming a negative pattern over and over and don't know why you're stuck? It's a shame wound. You've attached those negative patterns to your identity. It's no longer just an action; it's below that and connected to your being.

That's why you can't escape it. Because no matter where you go, there you are! The way out is through, and for this you have to gain awareness.

Why? Because only with awareness do you have the power to choose. How do you expand awareness?

1. Meditating, desiring to understand, constantly asking what's at the root of what you're thinking: "Why do I believe what I believe?"

2. Eating clean and in alignment with nature because your gut is tied to your mind and affects your clarity.

3. Spending time in the Bible, and letting God speak to you about you.

4. Spending time in a godly and wise community that's actually trying to help raise you up. Not raise you in terms of ego or pride but through soul. Giving you conviction and a mirror to see yourself more clearly.

5. Focusing on others more than just yourself. It's not about you, and helping others with their struggles helps you see the root of your own more clearly.

You have to choose to be curious. Choose to want to learn. And the first thing that allows you to make that choice is humility. Humility is a choice, and it's better to choose it than letting God choose it for you. It's not automatic but something we have to do with intention. It's something you have to choose every single day, and it's a battle.

I've dealt with pride so much in my life, and it sneaks up on you. You have no idea until you've looked around and realize, "Wow, I'm so disconnected from God."

You have to choose to submit yourself and look at where you could be blind. You can never become who you're meant to be unless you're willing to let go of who you are now. You have to be willing to surrender your identity and let go of the lies inside yourself. First admit, "Hey, I may have been lying to myself."

Let me shift your paradigm here. It's a good thing to discover where you're wrong because that means you can now grow and become better than who you've been. You can become more aligned with God.

Try it right now and ask yourself, "Where do I struggle to admit my faults or take ownership of failure in my life?" Let the answer come to you, and give yourself grace.

The Emotional Release Process

One of the best exercises you can do emotionally is this: When an emotion comes up inside of your body—when you feel triggered by a situation—I want you to use your awareness to analyze and just feel that emotion. Don't try to change it or figure it out too deeply. Just ask yourself, "Why is this here, and what is this emotion telling me?"

Go be alone if you need to. If you're feeling anger or sadness, make space to process it. If you need to, tell the people around you, "Hey, I'm feeling this. I need to go over here for a minute and process this."

Ask yourself: "Where do I feel this? Where's it speaking to me the most?"

You may feel it in your heart.

Maybe your gut.

It could even be your head.

Wherever it is, just put your awareness there.

As you sit with it, imagine that feeling is like a little child seeking attention. A good parent wouldn't say, "Hey, shut up," would they? Some might, but that tells you how they relate with themselves.

A good one would say, "Okay, what's going on? I want to sit through this with you. I'm going to be present with you."

The biggest issue and the biggest cause of sickness and disease—which is dis-ease—in our society is that people shut down their emotions and don't actually feel them, and they hurt relationships with themselves and others in the process. That energy stays stuck. It stays stagnant. Then it turns into disease in the body.

You have to sit still.

"Be still and know that I am God," like it says in Psalm 46:10. You need to let the Holy Spirit—that prompting feeling that's coming up, the conviction you feel internally—intercede on your behalf. When you feel those little tugs to go internally, that's the Holy Spirit guiding you, saying, "Hey, I'm helping you. I just need you to be present with what's going on right now and let me pray for you."

Feel that emotion and allow whatever comes up. Stop judging yourself for feeling a feeling. Is it evil to feel a feeling? Only if you think God is evil, because God feels feelings.

Any memories attached to it, any thoughts or beliefs attached, allow them to come up and don't judge them. Just witness them. As you go through it, ask yourself: "Is this actually true? The experience may be true, but is this really true?"

Feel that. Feel those beliefs and just let them be there without attaching your identity to them. Just notice them. As you notice them, you'll start to see these patterns, thought processes, and emotional patterns that come up.

You will get triggered again in the future, so don't think you won't. But now you have awareness, and the time to respond will expand from the newfound space. And through that awareness, again, you have the power of choice.

I want you to say that to yourself a few times:

"Through awareness, I have the power to choose."

"Through awareness, I have the power to choose."

"Through awareness, I have the power to choose."

The next time it happens, you'll have the ability to see, "Hey, this is an old belief coming up, and it's not actually true. I'm just going to sit with it and process it." As you sit and feel the emotion, maybe you need to cry it out and grieve it. Maybe you need to get angry and punch a punching bag or hit the gym. Express that emotion out however is needed, in a healthy way, and be with it while you do. If you Google the Latin etymology of *express* you will get to "press out" or "to represent."[1] Pressing out the trapped emotion is literally what you're doing, like oil from an olive, or wine from a grape. I don't think it's a coincidence that what's pressed out leads to arguably a better outcome than what it was before.

You're bringing your feeling to the surface and "squeezing it out" so that you can be purified. And through the other side of that, you'll be able to remove that block and have the clarity you need to see what you need to see.

The Foundation You Cannot Skip

I'll be straight with you: You may have gotten this book thinking that God is someone other than who he is—meaning, you may follow another faith. That's cool, but you need to get a Bible. You cannot see the truth without a Bible. I thought I did for so long, but that's because I was relying on what I thought was true rather than what the truth was. I've read countless other books, ranging from the Bhagavad Gita to the Torah, to the Hermetic Texts, Buddhism, and so on. I've studied these other paths while walking them.

You see this so much in the world today. There's an argument about "Oh, this is my truth." But just because it's your truth doesn't mean it's *the* truth.

We are children of God. We're fractals of the Whole, which means we can't see the whole thing unless we go to the Whole himself. We're only simple vantage points and made to embody that. There's

---

[1] "Etymology dictionary," EGW Writings, egwwritings.org, accessed November 25, 2025, https://m.egwwritings.org/en/book/14732.534573#34589.

a bunch of vantage points around us, and we need each other to see the whole truth, and to practice living out that truth, in love. That's why the body of Christ and the church are so important.

Imagine if a liver thought it could operate without a heart in the body, or a heart without a brain. The whole body would die. We are no different.

The Bible gives you the eyes to see this truth and the insights to see where you're missing the mark. That's the whole point of it. It's a book of transformation.

It feels against our nature to read it because our nature is to stay in allegiance to the body and the world. We want to have allegiance to the flesh, even if we say we don't. So, of course, everything in the Bible feels backward and controlling. If we're living in the flesh, the flesh is feeling controlled by God. It's not the spirit, because the spirit responds to and seeks God out.

The spirit has the fruit of self-control. The body does not want to control itself; it does everything to die. It's constantly wanting to feed itself more and more. It can't get enough because it's innately hollow without the spirit. Think about it. There's a vacuum in there without the spirit. So it's going to try to fulfill itself with something deeper that it just can't ever get or comprehend—because it's flesh and it's attracted to the counterfeit, fleshly versions of what your spirit is really searching.

So, read the Bible and let it convict you. When those emotions come up that may suck—those little convicting feelings—this is an opportunity to lean into them. The people with true humility are going to choose to do so, even if it sucks. You may feel unworthy in the process, and that's good. God is so holy that we are unworthy on our own, but worthy because he says we are. This perspective helps us put our worth in the right lens, not based on our own decision but because of God's.

Your ability to sit in silence and experience the truth and the pain that comes with that from a place of humility? That tells you how much your heart is actually in the journey of building a relationship with God and Jesus.

Your ability to let God's words kill your ego tells you your level of discipleship.

Learning to Talk to Someone You Can't See

The second thing you need to do is start praying. This was awkward for me at first because I was like, why would I pray to someone I can't even see? As I walked more of my journey and learned how to grow faith, I just threw out some Hail Marys. I thought, "Hey, God, I don't know if you're even there. But I'd love it if you make yourself known to me in a way that makes sense to me. That's clear. That I cannot miss. Because I've been missing a lot of things in my life."

Through that humility, there were different ways he made Himself known. Different experiences where I felt the power of the Spirit coming upon me. I experienced what felt like the gates of heaven opening up. I've experienced lust being fully taken out of my body. I've been used as a vehicle to help baptize people who I never thought would even consider having a relationship with Jesus, all while not even knowing why I was being used because I felt unworthy of it. Which we all are until God says otherwise.

Through prayers, what you're doing is not trying to say, "Hey, God, I want you to give me this and this and this." You're not trying to go shopping. He's not a genie. What you're doing is aligning yourself with his will. Every time you pray and focus on God and commune with him, you're aligning yourself with his will. Which gives you more peace, more clarity, and helps you see things in yourself.

Those prayers will be answered. He answers prayers that are in his will. So make sure you're praying every single day. Start your day first thing praying with God. Finish your day praying with God. He's got to be at the start and the end of everything—the Alpha and the Omega. Because that's going to determine the course of your life more than anything. He is your guidance system. Without him, you are absolutely lost.

There's nothing you can do without him. You can try, but you're not going to get very far. Eventually, you're going to feel like you're just forcing life. It's like trying to turn a wheel that has no power steering. It's just hard, and there's a lot of effort. You get tired of it eventually, and it starts to become painful.

Start praying. Start reading the Bible. Start spending time in God's presence regularly, even if it is just listening to worship music and taking it in. Focus on some quality about him—his mercy, his power, his grace, his love, or something else that resonates with you. Just focus on that and be in alignment with him. You cannot help but let it transform you if you keep your heart attached to him and focused on him above all things.

One of the frequent prayers I say out of habit now is, "God, help me make sure my heart's turned toward you. God, help me make sure my heart is turned toward you. Help me keep my heart humble and turned toward you. Help me have a soft heart and keep it turned toward you. I want to do your will above my own."

Even just saying that over and over helps maintain that connection. It also reminds you that you need to rely on him for your guidance.

The Fear That Keeps Us Stuck

I grew up thinking that it was scary to feel those sad emotions. If I expressed them, there would be a punishment for it. So I never took them to God. I thought if I admitted certain things to God—if I was honest about them—there would be some negative repercussions or punishment.

But as I learned throughout my journey that God loves me unconditionally and wants to be there with me as I go through it, as he's promised in the Bible, then even if I feel these things, God is with me as I go through it. He is guiding me through it. He's not going to leave me alone to the point that I get killed by it; only a part of myself will die. He's going to make sure I can feel exactly what I need to feel and handle right now so I can continuously move through trauma, through emotional blocks, and through any beliefs that may be holding me back.

We have to be willing to read the Bible, let it convict us, and give us the eyes to see. We can't rely on experience alone. Experience is a way for us to know firsthand if what we're living is true or not, like an experiment we're walking out. If we have an experience that is out of alignment with biblical truth, we're going to know. We're going to feel off in our body. We're going to feel gunky. We're going to feel dis-ease.

But if we're living something that is in alignment with the Bible and the truth, we're going to feel aligned, joyful, connected, and at peace. So you've got to start reading the Bible and using it as a map: "Am I actually living in alignment, or am I not?"

And it's not about getting anywhere or trying to do anything to get in alignment. It's about who you become. Who you're being right now. Your character.

The Space Where Miracles Live

When we start to gain the eyes to see from God, we no longer focus on what's missing. We can instead see how that space that is "missing" something is space for God to create a miracle in his timing. God fills the space in our life where we can't see what is happening because he is constant. He is never ending. He is always there.

I'm telling you right now—if you cannot see a good outcome, God is not yet finished in your life. If you're still breathing and waking up every single day, God is not done with you. He is still on your side because you've not yet finished the assignment he has planned for you. You've not walked out the destiny he is guiding you toward.

And if you have God, you have everything.

Once you clear out your blindness—once you take the mud off your glasses—that's when you can see clearly. This is when you can start to unlock the gift of vision and perceive life through the eyes of God.

We'll get into this next.

Chapter 1 Implementation: Week 2

Teaching Point

Your spiritual blindness isn't a character flaw—it's the result of emotional blocks and false beliefs you've carried since childhood. But here's the hope: What took years to build can begin dissolving the moment you're willing to feel what you've been avoiding.

Mindset Shift

From "I need to do more to see God" to "I need to remove what's blocking my sight."

Prayer

"Lord, I want to see. Remove the blocks in me that keep me blind— my shame, my pride, my fear, my unworthiness. Give me the humility to seek you with my whole heart and courage to face the things I've been avoiding. Open my eyes to see you, my ears to hear you, and my heart to know you as my Father. Amen."

Scriptures to Meditate On

- "Now faith is assurance of things hoped for, the conviction of things not seen" (Heb. 11:1 ESV).
- "Be still, and know that I am God" (Ps. 46:10 ESV).

- "Create in me a clean heart, O God, and renew a steadfast spirit within me" (Ps. 51:10 NKJV).

Action Steps

1. **Journal your blocks.** Write down the beliefs or emotions that keep you distant from God. Where do they come from?

2. **Sit with your emotions.** The next time you feel triggered, pause. Close your eyes. Ask: "Where do I feel this in my body? What is this emotion trying to teach me?"

3. **Start with scripture.** Read Hebrews 11:1 every morning this week. Ask God to help you "see the unseen."

CHAPTER 2 THE GIFT OF VISION

If you want to awaken your vision and perceive life through the eyes of God, here's the most important thing to remember. You have to ask yourself: "Do I just want his eyes, or do I want the God that comes with the eyes?"

One thing I've learned is that God will give you his eyes as a gift: "The hearing ear and the seeing eye, the Lord has made them both" (Prov. 20:12 NKJV). We're given ears to hear and the eyes to see, by God.

I repeat . . . by God.

By God. Not by ourselves. But you need to inquire in your heart if you're trying to actually get the gift alone, or the Giver of the gift with it.

In the story of the prodigal son, the son wanted to receive his inheritance but not the father who came with it. He gets his inheritance but immediately leaves home. He goes to a foreign land, where he squanders everything (Luke 15:11–32). God wants you to have the gift. He wants you to receive it, because it's aligned with his purposes and his character.

But because the son values the gift more than his father, he ends up losing everything. Then he realizes that he cannot do anything and needs to return home, that life is way better at home with his father. So he returns to his father, who he believes will reject him as unworthy and disgraceful. Instead, his father welcomes him back, running toward him with open arms.

The father welcomes him back with excitement and throws a party for him. The son realizes the most important thing is his relationship with his father.

You can get the eyes to see, but if you don't have God behind them, you're still going to be blind. You're not even going to be looking at things with the right motive. Your heart will not be in the right place.

You're going to want to use the eyes to deploy them into your own purposes, which, without God, are not aligned with love. You have to admit this truth to yourself first. You have to be willing to go to the roots of who you are to see it clearly.

At the end of the day, you can only give and receive love at the depth you've met yourself. And without that love, from the One who is love, you can't see fully.

The Superpower That Became My Trap

I remember when I first started experiencing spiritual vision, it felt like I'd unlocked a superpower. But slowly it started getting to my head, and small compromises crept in. I'd drift away from my time with God for work. Tell myself I didn't have enough time to be still. The gift was becoming more important than the Giver.

So to combat this, you first have to check the eyes of your heart. You can have eyes to perceive. Eyes to discern. But if your heart is not in the right place and you don't have the correct vision through your heart—how you see God and what you are loyal to—then you're not going to see correctly at all.

What you need to do is go back into your past. This is going to require brutal honesty with yourself. Do you truly love God as much as you think you do? Do you trust him as much as you think you do?

I used to be this person too. I thought I loved God. I really did. But I realized I didn't love God fully because I also was not obeying him; I only loved how I benefited from that halfhearted relationship.

Jesus said, "If you love me, keep my commands" (John 14:15 NKJV). So I realized, "I actually don't love God as much as I think, because I've been a freakin' rebel to the max." I thought by admitting that, there would be punishment. But in reality, what I gained was acceptance and belonging. An ability to see that he still loved me even when I didn't love him. That helped me see him as a loving Father instead of a distant boss in the sky.

That helped me gain true identity, and it started from looking at my heart.

Do you see the connection in all of what I've said so far? Are you seeing the pattern? This is a huge ingredient to gaining spiritual sight. Not just the importance of the heart being in the right place, but recognizing patterns too.

Pattern recognition is the ability to make a seen connection between something that was previously unseen. It's looking a layer deeper to see an invisible thread that connects two or more things together. This is how you will end toxic patterns in your relationships, your creations, and your mind.

You must ask yourself, "What is fundamentally the same between these things in front of me? What's at the root of them? What keeps repeating and showing up?"

This will train you to be able to do a few important things:

1. Anticipate the future in regard to the world around you.
2. Anticipate yourself and your own mind moving forward so that you can prevent yourself from making the same mistakes.
3. Be able to heal the past by seeing common occurrences that have popped up, and going back to the roots of them.

For the first point, being able to notice what's happening around you and linking it to a past occurrence can be both good and bad: good because it will protect you from getting stuck in another negative situation, and bad because you may be projecting your past into the future, and the negative situation you expected may not actually happen, so you self-sabotage.

That's why we go into the second point. This is where awareness comes in, which we will go into more detail about. When you see patterns, you can predict what's next, which means that when you focus on growing awareness of yourself, you'll be able to see the signs that lead to a certain pattern in your own thoughts.

This is how to rewire yourself. It's called metacognition, seeing your own mind and how you think. You must learn to be an architect of your own mind.

You want to look at your own habits, tendencies, and thought patterns, and ask yourself where they truly come from. Do they match God's law and character in the Bible? Because if the answer is yes, then they would be aligned with love.

Are they rooted in pride and fear? You may be about to self-destruct your blessings. It's important to take time out of our day to ponder these things and notice them in the moment as well as after the fact so you can learn.

Now for the final point. Let's keep it simple. If you can see patterns going forward, what does that mean you can see going backward? Hint: It starts with "patt" and ends with "erns." More *patterns*.

Follow the breadcrumbs back into the past, and you can finally reconcile the past by being present at the source. This is where you invite God in to help, and what I help guide people to do in their transformation journeys.

The Parent Connection You Can't Ignore

The past holds the key to our current identity due to the stories we've continually told ourselves. So let's go deeper . . .

What was your relationship like with your parents growing up? What is it like now?

Our parents are the first representations of God in our lives.

Were they distant? Were they overbearing? Did you feel like you had to earn their approval? Did you admire them or not? Did you feel like you had to perform for them?

I realized one day out of the blue that my bond with my dad was shared mostly through sports, actions, or achievements. Yes, we've had plenty of moments of hanging out, doing nothing. But I like to go deep emotionally, and he prefers not to as much—which is his choice. And that's fine. He carried a lot of weight while I was growing up and had to hold things together. To my young self, it felt like I was only half seen at times, so love was confusing.

If you have beliefs like this hidden inside of you, then you may have carried them your entire life and built it around how you think love has to be earned, similar to how I did. You haven't yet realized that there's only one constant in the entire universe: God's unconditional love.

His love is what transcends all things and all beliefs. It's the only thing you can truly hold on to with certainty and stability, and it melts away all of those false beliefs you've used to make sense of the world when you finally let him in.

If you felt like your entire life was unstable, or you felt insecure, or angry, or prideful, or you had to rely on yourself and couldn't fully lean on God, then you need to look at that relationship with your parents.

Maybe there's something you need to forgive in your heart. Maybe there's a story there to let go of that keeps you from seeing the love that's all around you. Maybe there's an area where you need to ask God to come in and help you feel the pain and grief you've not yet released.

Being willing to dive into our past stories is how we consciously choose to write our future ones.

Spiritual Eye Surgery

To get the vision you're looking for, you need to realize that it requires a spiritual surgery. You have to cut out what is sick and no longer able to be held. That starts in the heart.

Surgery requires knives. The truth itself is like a knife. It hurts you in a way to heal you. I had to feel the pain I didn't want to feel to allow myself to process what was at a deep level and move it out.

At the root of all of this is allowing yourself to feel feelings. It's very simple, but it's hard at the same time. Every false belief and stuck emotion is like poison that needs to be processed and evacuated.

Ask God to come into these areas. Give awareness to your heart where you feel pain or tension, where you feel struggle and energy. Close your eyes and just be in your body. Be in the stillness and feel where you feel those feelings, without judging.

When you think of core memories of your parents, where does the pain come up? When you think of key, emotionally charged moments, where do you experience it in the body? Do you feel it in your gut? Your heart? Your jaw? Do you feel it in your throat? Just gain awareness of those areas and ask yourself what is coming up here.

Our heart is usually linked to love. The gut, to gut feelings and confidence. The jaw, to tension and anger. The throat, to speaking truth. Each part of the body has a different purpose and story.

Talk to those areas like a little kid. Let God, through the Holy Spirit, guide you into those areas.

Remember, God never promised that you would never feel pain. But he did promise he will be with you as you go through it: "Even though I walk through the valley of the shadow of death, I will fear no evil, for you are with me" (Ps. 23:4 ESV).

Let the Spirit guide you into those areas and hang on to the trust that even if it sucks—even if you have to feel the heartbreak, even if you have to feel grief—God is with you, and he is the doctor behind the surgery table.

God is trustworthy. He will be with you this entire time. You can trust him. You have to trust his promises more than your own feelings, even when you're feeling them. You WILL be tempted not to... a lie doesn't trust what's true, after all.

The Hidden Wounds We All Carry

So go into the past and start to feel these things you have not felt before—the things you thought that if you encountered them, there would be punishment or pain that was just too unbearable.

Maybe you were silenced as a kid. Maybe you felt like you couldn't speak up or express yourself. Maybe you didn't know how to set a boundary. Maybe you felt helpless, or powerless, or worthless.

There are so many deep-rooted beliefs we have to look at internally. We need to encounter them and then admit to ourselves that they're there. We have to be honest and truthful because it's only through acceptance that we can get through to the courage that allows us to move forward.

Courage gets us to acceptance. But through acceptance, we can now get positive momentum because now we have the power of choice, created by neutralizing the past. We can see what's true without the emotional charge attached to it. Without the emotional charge, we can view things with wisdom.

But I do want to warn you: It *will* suck for a short time as you encounter the source of the pain. There's no sugarcoating it. Facing old, stagnant blocks of energy and emotion is not a fun process. But it becomes more enjoyable when you realize that on the other side of it is freedom.

Dive deep so you can fly high.

Rewiring Your Spiritual Vision

A lot of what we've covered so far is basic neuropsychology.

Why do I share this? Because if you don't have an understanding of how to think, the new thoughts being added to your brain will go to waste. You'll only use them at the capacity you're currently capable of, not at the capacity of what's possible.

Our brains have patterns internally, where we have emotions and experiences that have been repeated over and over throughout our entire life, stored in neural connections. They determine our beliefs, choices, preferences, personality, and more. We keep repeating them until we starve them out.

Think of the neurons in the brain as a highway. Imagine if you keep sending traffic down a certain road. Eventually, the road's going to have to be built out even more if it's being used a lot. It's going to have to be maintained. Because of that, there's going to be more traffic going through the road. What you need to do is divert traffic to a new pathway. In that process, you also have to starve out the one that has been getting used but no longer serves you.

That starts through your awareness, seeing these patterns and beliefs come up from the past. Instead of acting them out, you must engage them in a way so that you're just observing them happening. Through the observation, you can choose to take a different action.

Slowly, over time, you're going to rewire those thought patterns and start to see things in a different way. You have to be able to rewire your brain, or you will be a slave to circumstance. This is why Satan constantly wants to keep you chained to the past. You won't find freedom until you let go of it.

God is helping you do that, but it's your job to allow him to.

It starts through being able to feel the emotions that are blocking you so you can clear them out, and then choosing to fill your mind with new thoughts that are aligned with truth. This is why we meditate on and contemplate the Word of God. Every time we put more attention into what God says over what our past says, we get closer to the future he intended for us.

Read that again.

Start filling yourself with higher thoughts daily. As you walk, repeat to yourself verses that contradict the story you've told yourself about a certain situation. Do it in the car. Do it while you work. It doesn't matter where you do it; just do it. If you forget? Give yourself grace and start again.

Eventually, you will rewire your mind. When you change the way you see things, what you see will change. This mindset is the difference between being a victim or a victor.

The Conversations You're Avoiding

Out of all of the hard things we can do in life, I can say from experience, the hardest one is having a conversation we don't want to have.

I've done all of these psychotic adventure things in my life: climbing Kilimanjaro, suffocating in a temascal in El Salvador, and doing so much more. Yet it's always those "talks" we have with others that suck the most. And they're also the things I do that heal me the most.

Think of the body of Christ, humanity, as a literal body. Each person is a cell. If one cell goes rogue, what does that make it? Cancerous.

When we don't reconcile our relationships, we become cancerous to those around us. We become a breeding ground for bitterness and unforgiveness. Ironically, those are the feelings that contribute to sickness, though addictions, self-hatred, and more.

If you don't heal your relationships and come to harmony, you will get sick. I can almost guarantee it. I've seen it over and over in my line of work. Those who have bad relationships with themselves and others are usually the ones seeking the most healing.

So reconcile that past relationship with your parents. With friends. With your ex, even if internally. It may even require a conversation where you focus on just being honest about what you experienced, choosing to forgive them, and moving on.

Don't be tied to whether they accept it or not. Obviously, that's the goal, but they have free will. It's about God accepting the truth first, and foremost.

If you have a conversation with others, it may hurt them to hear what you have to say. It may also hurt you, depending on the situation. Their reactions may be tough. But God is going to be with you the entire time you do it. Maybe you have to have that hard conversation and express yourself. Listen—if they accept it with love, that's amazing. And if they don't? God still loves you. I want you to know that you will be okay.

I've had to do it myself. It's tough and scary. I avoided the "talks" so much my entire life. Sometimes you need to do it gently; sometimes you've just got to rip the Band-Aid off. Both suck; it just depends on how you like it! (As well as what the situation calls for.)

Wondering if you'll be rejected, abandoned, or betrayed is a part of the journey that allows you to keep coming home to God. You have to face the pain, but in that pain, he will turn his face to you.

Expanding Your Spiritual Awareness

The best way to expand your awareness so you can receive more insights and receive what God is saying to you is, of course, to read the Bible. You want to feel convictions come up inside of you, as if God is coaching you from the inside out, because he is. Let him speak to you as a loving Father. But as he speaks to you, you want to sit still and internalize it. Acknowledge what you're feeling, and don't run away. We need to turn and face the music, even if it doesn't sound appealing in the moment.

When I read the Bible, I can get a conviction that causes pain, frustration, anger, or sadness. I can also get one that gives me joy and confirmation. Both are good. After that, I'll just let it move through me and soak it in.

I'll close the book for a bit and sit still, or go for a walk. I'll ask God to bring the feeling up to the surface so I can sit with it, or if I'm on the move, I'll keep the focus on where I'm feeling the feeling inside of me and what it's saying.

This is meditation. So many people in Christianity are scared of meditation because there's been the connotation of a new age way of thinking attached to it. *Meditation* is just a word. The word itself is not going to hurt you. Meditation is a deep pondering and an awareness of something.

The goal is not to just clear our mind but to renew our mind: "Do not conform to the pattern of this world, but be transformed by the renewing of your mind" (Rom. 12:2 NIV). From my experience, clearance is required so that we can have space for something fresh.

But it comes from washing it with the Word as well, "that he might sanctify and cleanse her with the washing of water by the word" (Eph. 5:26 NKJV).

Imagine trying to put new furniture in your house on top of old furniture. That's just stupid, and it doesn't make any sense. For renewal, we have to first meditate on the feelings and thoughts going on in our body and mind. We have to again encounter ourselves and go to the root of what's happening internally, inviting God in. We have to wash the inside of the cup, as Jesus describes to the Pharisees (Matt. 23:26). When we clean the inside of the cup, we go through the process of feeling the emotion in our body, asking it to come to the surface, expanding the awareness of why we feel things in the first place. Then, in that new space, we fill our minds with a new thought, and it's so much easier to discern what is and isn't God.

The Samurai Method That Changed Everything

Each day, meditate for a short time by silencing yourself and feeling those emotional blocks or movement in your body. Just be more still.

Whether it's starting with ten minutes, or twenty minutes, or even getting up to an hour—focus on being in your body every single day. Be present with it and feel it. Your body is the vehicle and vessel that carries you through life. If you aren't self-aware, you're always going to miss the signals your body is constantly trying to tell you. It's one of the main ways you listen to God, how you *receive* from God.

It is the temple that the Spirit resides in: "Do you not know that your bodies are temples of the Holy Spirit?" (1 Cor. 6:19 NIV).

One of the meditation methods I learned in college was the Samurai meditation method from a book by Richard L. Haight called *The Warrior's Meditation*. It was not Christ focused, but it was a great vehicle to grow my awareness.

Pause: I want to say this really quick. So many people who follow Christ are scared to read books that do not necessarily revolve around Christ. That's a cover-up for fear, and if you read the book of Daniel in the Bible, you will see that he was strong in faith, so he was able to read Babylonian literature and gain cultural wisdom to help him succeed in his endeavors. Don't let anyone convince you that it's evil to learn from others. Just stay connected and loyal to Jesus above all so that you have the right lens to view from. Anyway, back to it.

Reading that book, I learned how to expand my peripheral vision and do what the samurai warriors would do to meditate and increase their awareness. If a samurai went into battle thinking instead of flowing, he'd get his head chopped off. He needed to be in flow state, where intuition takes over.

We live in a culture of chronic overthinking and cerebral overkill. In my junior year of college, I would practice this everywhere, especially in class when I wasn't paying attention. I'd do it walking between classes. I'd do it in the gym—which felt like my temple, to a degree. The gym became my laboratory for consciousness.

This method helps you get into an alpha-brain-wave state—flow state—versus beta, which is what you feel when you're caffeinated and hyperfocused. So you need to work on expanding your vision, both literally and energetically.

As you do your next task today, or even right now, start trying to see out of your peripheral vision. Breathe into your body. Feel into your body. Look forward at a point while also trying to expand your peripheral vision.

Let's try it together. Read this line of text, and as you do it, I want you to try and see as far out to the side of you as you can while tracking each word on the page, still keeping it in focus. Try and find a point where you can see outside of yourself and in front of yourself. It should feel like your awareness "backs up" inside of your head. It may feel straining for a second, but it will relax if you relax into it.

As you see these words from that perspective, I want you to now also breathe with your belly, from the diaphragm.

Breathe this full sentence in.

Now all the way out.

Now in again, all the way, connecting to it.

Now out again, still holding that view in your peripheral and seeing the words.

And that's it. Eventually, you add in all of the senses, but it's that simple.

We aren't taught basic things like this because we live in the mind and want to overcomplicate everything. Simplicity is scary because it shows us how blind we've been.

The more you do this, the more you take in your full field of view. Allow yourself to take in more of the world around you and connect deeply to it, while remaining detached from it and connected to yourself.

Then start noticing what sounds come up. Don't attach yourself to the sounds but just observe them. Next, notice what you're smelling. With any scents that come up, same thing. Next, tastes. Next, feelings.

Eventually, as I practiced this, I started to see all my thoughts more clearly, just as a result of being conscious of how I interacted with reality. You get to the point where you can start to feel one with the environment around you. You can feel the subtlety more. You can start to feel how God is moving in creation.

Jesus was the embodiment of a true man, but he was also the most sensitive of all. Imagine being connected to the Father, who knows everything, and also knowing everyone's thoughts and feelings. That's deep sensitivity.

To see God clearly, you must first learn to see yourself clearly. Otherwise, you'll be viewing from an extremely limited lens. The reverse also works, when God makes his presence manifest to you in a way that destroys your perception of everything.

The Awareness Alarms

Here's another practice that rewired my brain: Set three random alarms throughout each day on your phone. Every time an alarm goes off, ask yourself three questions: "Who am I? Where am I? What am I doing?"

I call these awareness check-ins. You need to check in with yourself and your environment. This trains your brain to be more present and aware of what's going on. This trained my brain to constantly check in with itself until it became automatic, a habit of becoming aware. If our mind is constantly focused on the future or stuck in the past—if our brain is anywhere other than right here—we're going to miss how God is moving around us in each moment.

Before we even try to get the vision from God—which, again, is a gift that comes through a relationship with him—we have to first cultivate that relationship with him in the here and now, in the present moment. That requires us to be right here right now so we can see him, so we can feel him.

Not someday. Not tomorrow. Now.

God is always speaking to us in some way, even in the silence. It's whether we allow ourselves to see him or hear him that's the personal choice.

After some time of doing these exercises, I started to feel the difference. Then there was one night when everything changed.

I was lying in bed, looking at the ceiling fan, doing some awareness practices and pondering some deep esoteric concepts and ideas. Out of nowhere, as I was looking at the fan, I have no other words to say other than I became one with the ceiling fan. I had an experience of complete unity, where everything made sense, and it was like the gates of heaven opened up. It felt like a wave of ecstasy took over my being. I was connected to everything in a sea of pure grace and felt intertwined with existence itself. I felt deeply in tune with my heart as tears rolled down my cheeks. I was surrounded and touched by a deep peace, leading to a deepening of emotional capacity.

I will never forget that experience. It was nothing I forced, but it was given as a gift. All of the moments of darkness I experienced up to that point had happened for a reason.

We have to feel the darkness fully to understand light. It's only through the valley of the shadow of death that we find who we are and whose we are.

Remember—the gift of vision will be given to you. But you have to ask yourself: "Am I someone who can hold the gift? Or am I going to be like the prodigal son, who squanders it and has to find my way back home? Am I truly seeking with all of my heart?"

If you can first focus on being the person who can hold the gift being given to you—through being present, through being aware, through listening and seeing what is going on around you naturally, and through tuning in to the subtlety of your heart—then God can lean on you to give you his sight. You *can* have a better relationship with him. He *wants* that with you.

He can see when you're ready if you're doing the work to look at your heart and listen to the convictions he's giving you. He is so graceful and generous. Take time to sit and think about all the things he's done in your life that you didn't deserve for any reason other than him saying so. Let that stir your heart in gratitude.

He wants to make his presence known to you, because he's already there trying to, and he lives within you. You just have to meet him there. As God says, "You will seek me and find me, when you search for me with all of your heart" (Jer. 29:13 NKJV).

Surrender to that truth, and let it be your guide.

Chapter 2 Implementation: Week 3

Teaching Point

Once you've identified what's blocking you, here's the truth: Spiritual sight is a gift that comes through relationship, not achievement. You can't earn God's eyes through perfect meditation or spiritual gymnastics—you receive them by becoming present enough to hold what he's already trying to give.

Mindset Shift

From "I need to master spiritual techniques" to "I need to be present with the Giver of sight. Close vicinity is the prize."

Prayer

"Father, I don't just want your gifts—I want you. Give me eyes to see you, not just your blessings. Help me reconcile my past, especially my relationship with my parents, friends, and anyone else who I've known, so I can see you as you truly are. Guide me through the spiritual surgery needed to remove what blocks my vision. Teach me to be present, to be aware, to receive what you're already speaking. I trust you to be with me through the pain. In Jesus's name, amen."

Scriptures to Meditate On

- "If you love me, keep my commands" (John 14:15 NIV).
- "You will seek me and find me, when you search for me with all your heart" (Jer. 29:13 NKJV).
- "Do you not know that your bodies are temples of the Holy Spirit?" (1 Cor. 6:19 NIV).

Action Steps

1. **Parent inventory.** Write a letter to your parents (whether you send it or not). Be honest about how their love shaped your view of God's love and what you've learned from them. Seal it with gratitude and forgiveness.

2. **Samurai practice.** For the next week, practice peripheral-vision meditation for ten minutes daily. Expand your awareness to include all five senses. Notice how your perception shifts. Do it while working and sitting.

3. **Awareness alarms.** Set three random alarms on your phone. When they go off, ask: "Who am I? Where am I? What am I doing?" Journal any patterns you notice going on in your mind. In a week, reflect.

Check my YouTube @masonkuhr for the samurai meditation video I posted.

Checking In

Do not go to the next chapter until you implement these action steps for one week. I want you to transform, not just accumulate. If you skipped last week, clean it up for this week and moving forward.

CHAPTER 3 SURRENDER—THE DOORWAY TO TRUE SIGHT

For most of my life, I was self-reliant. I am still moving through that, but it was a whole different level—like an "Alexander the Great" level.

I wasn't self-reliant in the sense that I denied God existed or didn't believe in him. I knew God had blessed me. I could see his hand in my successes. But here's the subtle deception I lived under: I thought he blessed me because I put in the effort, not because of his character or that things aligned with his plans for me.

I wanted everything he had to give me except himself. I thought God was some cosmic vending machine. I put in the work; he dispensed the blessing. I showed up; he showed out. I planted; he gave increase.

It seemed like a fair exchange, a divine partnership where I was the senior partner and Divine Daddy in the sky blessed me because I was "a dawg," in my own language. It was a very narcissistic relationship on my end!

I really wanted God to bless *my* plans above everything. Not surrender to his plans. Not seek his will. Just take my blueprints, stamp them with divine approval, and make them succeed. I wanted him to be my cosmic cosigner, not my Lord.

And honestly? It worked. For twenty-five years, it worked.

Until May of 2024, when everything I built started crumbling like a sandcastle at high tide. And my illusion of self-confidence crumbled with it.

The Peak of Self-Reliance

Starting in May of 2024, I experienced an avalanche of pride destruction that validated every wrong belief I had about success up to that point. I had made more money than I'd ever made in my life, and it felt like it was out of thin air.

My supplement brand, the Stampede Network, had gone through a rough previous six months, trying to recover from a random virality wave that shocked our supply chain at the end of 2023. It's a blessing to sell your product until you lose half your subscribers . . . but that's a different story, and this isn't a business book.

I finally was able to lead back our momentum, and we were extremely close to cracking our first million-dollar month. It was sickening how fast money came in and then went out to pay for expenses. I was so numb to it, but I also felt like a conqueror. It was the kind of money that makes you feel invincible, and scared of losing it at the same time.

I felt like I had brought my business back from the dead through sheer force of will. We were on a charge, like Alexander the Great, crushing everything in sight. Every campaign we launched hit again.

Every move we made multiplied, finally, after months of frustration and recovery.

But I was too aggressive at the time. Unhinged. The success made me reckless with a thirst for redemption. Like a drunk driver who hasn't crashed yet, I was worshiping my own skill and will, but hanging on a thread without realizing it.

I got too comfortable in the chaos. I started drinking too much caffeine just to maintain the manic pace. My sleep schedule was destroyed. Every day was random, with no routine, no structure, no rhythm. Just pure momentum and adrenaline. My relationship was suffering, too, as a by-product.

Get up, go to the gym, conquer. That was about it. I didn't care about much else, and I thought that was what an honorable man would do. It felt like I was listening to EDM in my brain, even though nothing was playing.

Constant noise. Constant motion. Constant conquest.

My thoughts raced at a thousand miles per hour. My body vibrated with fight-or-flight. I was a human *doing*, not a human *being*.

Looking back, I can see the warning signs. The way my hands would shake from too much stimulation. The way I'd snap at people who couldn't keep up with my pace. The way I'd lie in bed at night with my heart pounding, unable to turn off the machine I'd become, waking up in a pool of sweat.

But in the moment? I thought God was blessing my hustle. I thought he was rewarding my grind. I thought this was what favor looked like.

I was wrong.

I couldn't see that my business was a reflection of me: successful and big on the outside, but a chaotic mess internally. It was like a house of cards with an unstable foundation, waiting to fall. But sometimes God has to break us to make us.

I had no idea the mental torment that would lie in front of me and the depths of myself that were about to be exposed.

The Hidden Idol

But there was another god I was serving that was even more deceptive than success. Her name was love. Or at least, what I thought was complete love from a human perspective.

My relationship that led me to Jesus was the most transformative of them all.

She was the first woman I'd met who helped me understand what love felt like, at a higher capacity than we'd both experienced. After years of surface-level relationships and performative connections, she showed me more depth than I had seen. She showed me more vulnerability. She showed me what it meant to be seen and still accepted.

And without realizing it, I made her my god.

I worshiped how she felt about me more than how God felt about me. Her moods became my storms. Her approval became my oxygen. Her love became my religion. When she was happy with me, I felt blessed. When she was distant, I felt cursed. My entire emotional and spiritual climate was determined by another human being.

I was confusing human love, which changes like the weather, with God's love, which is constant like gravity.

The thing about making a person your god is that they're not equipped for the job. No human can bear the weight of another person's worship. It's too heavy. It warps them. It warps you. It warps the relationship into something it was never meant to be.

I wasn't firm in God's love for me, so I tried to find that firmness in her. But human emotions fluctuate. They have bad days, they have hormones, they have their own struggles and fears and insecurities. When you make someone's emotions your god, you're building your house on shifting sand.

God's love never changes like people can. It's something we can't even put into words because he *is* love. Real love. Not that he has love or gives love—he *is* love itself (1 John 4:8). Unchanging. Unwavering. Unaffected by your performance or problems.

He was always showing up for me, in ways I couldn't comprehend based on what I felt I deserved. But I couldn't see that. I was too busy worshiping at the altar of human affection.

When the Music Stopped

After May of 2024, everything started to fall apart. And I mean *everything.*

It was like every single thing I tried to do hit an invisible wall. The same strategies that printed money produced nothing. The same energy that moved mountains now couldn't move pebbles. I was throwing everything at the wall—videos, ads, content, new products, new funnels, new everything. Nothing was sticking.

But it wasn't just the business. The relationship—my secret god—started showing cracks too. What had felt like heaven started feeling like pressure. What had been effortless became forced. The very thing I'd been worshiping started feeling heavy.

The rest of 2024 became a master class in divine demolition. God was systematically removing every false foundation I'd built my life on, and every way I'd related with things out of harmony, with love.

No matter what I had put out in the business, nothing got results. It felt like supernatural resistance and an infinite plateau. Like every door was being deliberately closed. Like every effort was being divinely frustrated.

I felt disconnected from everything and everyone, stuck in obligation and routine. I still hadn't brought my business partner on full-time, so I was carrying the full weight of the team while being completely unaware of my own destructive patterns.

My ambition had made me blind. But worse than that, my idolatry had made me deaf to God's voice.

The weight was crushing. Not just the weight of responsibility, but also the weight of confusion. Why wasn't anything working? Why did everything feel like I was pushing a boulder uphill, only to watch it roll back down? Why did every area of my life feel like it was falling apart simultaneously?

My relationship was hard—constant conflict, constant tension. We were speaking different languages, wanting different things. The person who was supposed to be my peace had become another source of stress, simply reflecting my own. The god I'd made her into was failing to save me. I couldn't see how all of this started with me.

My fitness fell apart. The discipline I'd once prided myself on evaporated. I'd skip workouts to take another meeting that went nowhere. I'd eat garbage because I was too stressed to cook. My body, which had been a temple, became a storage unit for cortisol and stimulants.

Everything in my life felt like force. Like trying to breathe underwater. Like running in a dream where I couldn't move fast enough, no matter how hard I tried.

It was exhausting, but God let me break down so I could break through.

The Vine and the Branches

Looking back, I see that I had to face the uncomfortable truth. I was completely out of character and integrity. I was not in alignment with God's will. And you have to be in alignment with God's will to be fruitful: "I am the vine; you are the branches. Whoever abides in me and I in him, he it is that bears much fruit, for apart from me you can do nothing" (John 15:5 ESV). Those words hit different when you're experiencing the "nothing" part firsthand.

I wanted to be a free-agent branch doing its own thing, because I didn't want to feel controlled by being attached to a vine. Unfortunately, I didn't realize that would kill me. I thought I could have the fruit without the root. The blessing without the relationship. The provision without the surrender. I wanted God to water my independent branch while I grew wherever I pleased.

I was slowly dying, slowly poisoning myself through lack of integrity and character. Not fully aligned with God's will. I was half in, half out. I was lukewarm: "So, because you are lukewarm—neither hot nor cold—I am about to spit you out of my mouth" (Rev. 3:16 NIV). Being lukewarm feels like drowning in shallow water. You're not deep enough to swim but not shallow enough to stand. You're in this horrible middle ground where nothing works. Too spiritual for the world to embrace you fully. Too worldly for God to use you powerfully.

I was distant and alone, even in crowded rooms. Like I was constantly getting punished by life for a crime I didn't know I'd committed. My daily choices were frantic and aggressive. I'd wake up swinging, attacking the day like it was an enemy to be conquered rather than a gift to be received.

The thing about being lukewarm is that you don't realize it's happening. You think you're balanced. You think you're being wise by keeping one foot in the kingdom and one foot in the world. You tell yourself you're being strategic, practical, smart.

But we're really just being cowardly, to be blunt. Too scared to fully commit to God. Too scared to fully commit to the world. So we live in this gray purgatory where nothing works because you're not hot enough for God to fully use you and not cold enough for the world to reward you.

It's not even about what you're doing as much as how your heart is positioned. Where does it find itself loyal to? And how much? This is what to ask yourself.

The Divine Chess Match

I had to go through this painful journey where I was fighting reality over and over. Like a boxer who doesn't know the fight is already over, I kept swinging at air.

I was trying so freaking hard, harder than I'd ever tried in my life. Working twelve-hour days, sometimes seven days a week. Pouring everything I had into saving what was dying. Nothing was working. When God decides that something is going to happen, it's going to happen.

Do you know what it feels like to give everything you have and get nothing in return? To pour out your soul and watch it evaporate? To plant seeds with blood and sweat, only to harvest dust? I know you do. We all do. It absolutely sucks, and it drains you.

Then came the moment of clarity. The divine revelation wrapped in pain. I realized God was using this. All of it. The failure. The frustration. The force that led nowhere.

That was him saying, "All right, son, you've had a lot of success in your own efforts, but you've separated from me. Now I'm going to have to bring you home."

God was pruning me, taking away the blessings and things I was experiencing so I could have a relationship with him, so that I would be reliant on him and worship him instead of worshiping my own creation and the created things of this world. John 15:2 ESV states, "Every branch in me that does not bear fruit he takes away, and every branch that does bear fruit he prunes, that it may bear more fruit."

He was removing my false gods, one by one. First the money. Then the momentum. Then the confidence. Then the relationship stability. Like a divine surgeon, he was cutting away everything I'd used to replace him. And the irony of it all is that I was making the choices that led to these things, but I had absolutely zero clue what that meant.

The Cost of Multiple Gods

The thing about having multiple gods in your life is that they go to war with each other, but they equally want to steal your attention. My god of success demanded all my time. My god of relationship demanded all my attention. My God—the real God—was getting whatever scraps were left.

I'd wake up and check my bank account before I'd talk to God. I'd text my lady good morning before I'd tell him good morning. I'd plan my day around revenue and external relationships, squeezing in a quick prayer if I had time.

He was not a first thought. He was a second thought. And I was not doing the best job at living out Matthew 6:33 ESV: "But seek first the kingdom of God and his righteousness, and all these things will be added to you."

The hierarchy was clear:

1. Acquisition and work
2. Romantic relationship
3. God

And God, in his jealous love, said "No more." But to me it sounded like absolutely nothing, because I was deaf.

God says, "You shall have no other gods before me" (Exod. 20:3 ESV), not because he is insecure, but because he knows that anything else we worship will eventually destroy us. He's not trying to limit us—he's trying to liberate us from things that can't bear the weight of our worship.

Money makes a terrible god. It promises security but delivers anxiety. It promises freedom but creates bondage. It promises happiness but produces emptiness. And when the market crashes or the business fails, your god dies and takes your identity with it. It feels like a never-ending goalpost that keeps getting pushed back and always feels like it's going to fall apart. Money isn't alive until we give it a purpose to serve us with, so how can it lead us?

Human love makes an even worse god. It promises completion but reminds you of your incompleteness. It promises constancy but changes with emotions. It promises to fill the God-shaped hole in your heart, but it's the wrong shape—like trying to plug a circular hole with a square peg. No matter how hard you push, it won't fit. It only leaves you hurting what you wanted to love, because the human on the other side of your devotion isn't meant to live with that responsibility.

Your girlfriend or boyfriend, husband or wife, cannot be your Father (or mother). And you can't be theirs either.

The Breaking Point

The biggest breaking point for my business, but also the most freeing, came on an ordinary day that became anything but ordinary. My business partner had reached his limit. I could sense it in him—that combination of exhaustion, frustration, and resignation that comes when someone's been carrying too much for too long and gets tired of feeling stuck in place. He told me he wanted to talk about something that was on his mind, and scheduled a call.

We sat across from each other on video chat, me sitting in my home office, the same setting where I'd celebrated our biggest wins. It now felt like an ultimatum was right around the corner.

He laid it out straight: He couldn't keep going like this. Something had to change. The business needed restructuring. He needed more ownership, more recognition, more say in decisions. He'd been carrying responsibilities without the authority or equity to match, mostly because of my own inability to let go of control.

I felt my chest tighten while my heart started to pick up speed. Everything in me wanted to hold on tighter. To maintain control. To keep things the way they were. Greed whispered in my ear about percentages and profits. Pride reminded me who built this. Fear painted pictures of what I'd lose if it all fell apart.

But deeper than all of that, exhaustion spoke truth. I couldn't carry all the weight anymore. My shoulders were breaking from carrying it. My soul was fracturing from not living in flow. My body was failing. Something had to give, and it couldn't be my sanity.

He had looked over our finances, and even if they looked great on the surface or in the eyes of someone staring at revenue, the back end looked like a hurricane had given them a visit. I had my hands, eyes, and heart in so many things that I was completely blind to how the business was operating in the first place.

As he shared the numbers with me, all I could think to myself was, "Wow, I am definitely not meant to be the main finance guy of this whole thing." It was bad, embarrassing, and humorous at the same time. It was a reflection of my chaotic inner world.

Then, my now full-time partner and also one of my best friends, then told me his terms that he needed to continue, or he'd have to do his own thing. I respected what he said, and I deeply valued him and everything we'd gone through.

In that moment, I had to choose. Hold on to it all and likely lose everything, including the depth of relationship with a friend and partner who said that it wouldn't be taken personally, yet there was still always that twinge of not feeling valued. Or I could let go and trust God with the outcome.

So I did the right thing and brought him on full time. I surrendered control of owning my "baby" so that we could parent together. If you haven't started a business before and been through that situation, you may not fully understand, but if you know you know. Surrendering control is the entrepreneur's worst fear.

Yet for me, it ended up being the best business decision I've ever made. I had to have my way ripped out of my hands before I could willingly grab onto God's.

That conversation was God performing surgery on my grip. Each word was a scalpel cutting away my white-knuckled control. Each moment of silence was like an antiseptic burning away infection. It hurt to see the situation for what it was. But wow, it was healing.

The Unwilling Student

I wish I could give you a clean formula for surrender, like:

Step one: Read this verse.

Step two: Pray this prayer.

Step three: Experience breakthrough.

But surrender doesn't work like that. Surrender is messy. It's ugly. It's everything in you screaming "no" while your spirit whispers "yes." It's dying while you're still alive. It's letting go while every instinct tells you to hold tighter.

For me, surrender has always come when being faced with a decision that has required me to let go of something, or some way of doing things, that I'd known my whole life. The only "formula" is choosing to be humble in those moments, seeking God above all things.

But even those can feel distant when you're in the thick of it. When your life is falling apart and someone quotes Romans 8:28 at you, you want to throw something at their head.

What I've realized is that some of us need surrender forced upon us unfortunately. We're too strong-willed for our own good. Too capable. Too resourceful. And that's not to sound prideful, but it is simply reality.

We'll always find a way to maintain control until God lovingly backs us into a corner where control is no longer an option and we have to face ourselves in a spiritual time-out. He has to arrange circumstances where surrender isn't a choice but a necessity. Like a divine chess Lord, he positions the pieces of our lives until the only move left is to tip our little king so we can replace it with the big one.

For twenty-six years, I'd been asking God to bless my plans: "God, here's what I'm going to do. Please make it successful. Here's who I'm going to love and how I'm going to do it. Please make it work. Here's who I'm going to be. Please endorse it."

But God isn't interested in being my assistant. He's not applying for the position of cosmic helper. He's God. He has his own plans. And they're better than mine, even when they require me to let go of everything I'm gripping.

To see those plans clearly, you have to choose with your heart to want to see them.

The Violence of Love

God allowed Satan to tempt me. He allowed pain so that I would come into a relationship with him, just like with Job: "The Lord gave and the Lord has taken away; may the name of the Lord be praised" (Job 1:21 NIV).

That verse hits differently when you're the one doing the losing. I can't give Satan all of that credit, though. A lot of it was me simply being disobedient and dumb.

But here's what I learned: God's removal is his mercy. What feels like punishment is actually protection. What feels like loss is actually preparation for greater gain. He takes away the good to give you the best. He removes what you want to provide what you need.

My success had become my god. My ability had become my identity. My relationship had become my religion. My creation had become my cult. So God, in his violent love, had to tear down the altars I'd built to everything except him.

Think about it. How else could he get my attention? I wasn't listening in the success. I wasn't seeking him in the abundance. I wasn't humble in the victory. I wasn't surrendered in the romance. So he had to speak in the only language I'd understand—loss.

He let my business crumble for a time to show me he's my provider, and that only through a stable relationship with him can I have stability in other things.

He let my relationship struggle to show me that he's my first and main love.

He let my strength fail to show me that he's my power.

He let everything I trusted collapse to show me that he's the only solid foundation.

You can do nothing without God (John 15:5). This is the hard fact we all have to accept if we want a better, different life.

The Confession That Changes Everything

One way to willingly surrender is to look at your heart and see where your motive really is. What are you truly worshiping? What gets your first thoughts in the morning and your last thoughts at night? What makes you feel secure? What would devastate you to lose?

Be honest with yourself. Brutally honest. Where is your emotional center based?

For me, it was the business and the relationship. The money and the woman. The success and the romance. These weren't just things I had—they were who I was. My identity was so wrapped up in being a successful entrepreneur, in being in a beautiful relationship, that I couldn't imagine who I'd be without them.

I thought those were what made me worthy of my Father's love. And that's exactly why they had to be surrendered. They were created by a wounded version of me, and they had to die and be reborn.

Do not worry if the answer to what you're worshiping is painful. Do not worry if it's not God, unless you refuse to give it over to him and let him tell you what's up. Then you should definitely think things over a bit. But like a lot of people, I used to think admitting the truth to God would lead to punishment. Like he was waiting for me to slip up so he could smite me. I simply hadn't experienced his perfect love.

But in reality, he already knows. He's not waiting for your confession so he can punish you. He's waiting for your confession so he can heal you. Ever ask yourself why Jesus, being God, asks people questions probably (definitely) already knowing the answer? It's for the one getting asked, not himself. He wants to redeem you and restore you, so you can experience him as your Dad. He loves you so much that he's willing to let you hate him temporarily if it means saving you eternally.

Take that truth you're scared of saying to God. Say out loud what you've been too scared to admit. Tell him you don't know what you're doing, that you need his help. You need his guidance, and you can't do it alone.

Say this out loud and remember there's power in verbal confession: "I've been trying to be the god of my own life, and I'm failing. I've been worshiping my own ability, and it's killing me. I've been making [her or him] my god, and it's destroying both of us. I've been half in and half out, and I'm drowning in the shallow end. Help me. Save me. I surrender."

After this, feel what comes up. Connect to it and see it for what it is. This is how you'll be able to accept it and change your situation.

The Death of the False Self

If you want to discover who you truly are, spend time in the Bible seeking the wisdom of Scripture over your own understanding: "Trust in the Lord with all your heart and lean not on your own understanding; in all your ways submit to him, and he will make your paths straight" (Prov. 3:5–6 NIV).

If you wanted to see in yourself who God sees, why would you view yourself from your own vantage point? This is how to start to gain separation between the true and the false versions of you.

But here's the thing—in my experience, I also had to go through the pain of having circumstances arranged by God so that I would willingly surrender to that. Some of us are too stubborn for gentle conviction, and we like who we see, even if it's not healthy. We need aggressive intervention to take us away from pride.

God orchestrated a master class in letting go, and I was the unwilling student who had to repeat the course until I learned the lesson. It meant surrendering to life itself. Surrendering to the lessons and emotions and all the experiences that came up. Not judging them as good or bad but seeing that they were all taking me closer to God.

That conclusion took me a long time to come to. For most of my life, I saw downfalls as the universe trying to spite me and would take my ultimate revenge to get them back.

You don't see it in the moment, though. In the moment, it's easy to keep living out that same story as the "hero" who needs to fix everything, keeping you from fully trusting. Your knuckles are white. Your jaw is clenched. Your whole body is rigid with the effort of holding on. And it completely sucks.

When you have had enough, and the holding on starts to destroy your soul, you finally let go. Your false self, the one that served you for a time but no longer, goes away with it.

Every loss feels like death because, in a way, it is. You're dying to who you were. Dying to what you wanted. Dying to the life you planned. Dying to the identity you created. Dying to the gods you made your master. And nobody wants to die, even when resurrection is promised on the other side.

But when you're rooted in Christ, you at least have room for hope.

The Anatomy of Resistance

There's a tendency to want to shut down or suppress the emotions that come with surrender. To go numb to the experience. To find a bottle, a pill, a person, or a project to distract you from the pain. Your body has a thousand ways to avoid feeling what needs to be felt.

You may spend 99 percent of your day convincing yourself you don't have any underlying issues, which actually takes you away from being led into transformation.

I tried it all. More caffeine to push through the fatigue. More work and sex to avoid the emotions. More planning to avoid the surrender. More activity to avoid the stillness where God speaks.

But you must go through those feelings; you can't go around them.

It's only through feeling the feeling completely and then looking back in hindsight that you can acquire wisdom. Wisdom is a lesson learned without the emotional experience attached to it. It's just the truth that's left over once your mind is no longer fighting reality. It's the skeleton that remains after the flesh of emotion has decomposed. Clean, clear, and undeniable.

That's why wisdom is a gift. You experience life and gain a higher perspective. When it's all said and done, you're truly seeking to learn. When you're in the middle of the pain, you can't see the purpose. When you're in the middle of the loss, you can't see the lesson. When you're in the middle of the dying, you can't see the resurrection. Or at least, it's really hard unless you're fully grounded in God, but even then, he can feel distant.

When you can't feel the Teacher with you, how can you possibly learn? That's where it gets tricky, and it becomes a game of trust. But on the other side, when the emotional charge has dissipated, the wisdom remains like gold refined by fire.

This is why the ultimate baptism is not just by water, but by fire.

The Lessons Written in Scar Tissue

One of the biggest lessons I learned was realizing that I can't change people. For years, I tried. I thought if I just loved harder, worked smarter, or communicated better, I could transform the people around me into who I needed them to be.

With romance, I thought my love could heal wounds. My consistency could cure fears. My dedication could dissolve doubts. I was trying to be a savior when she already had one, and ironically, I was making things worse. I was trying to be her god when she needed me to just be human and stay connected to the one and only God. Since I had an imperfect relationship with him, I didn't love correctly.

I extended relationships way past their expiration date. Not everyone is meant to keep going with you if they're also not willing to level up or go in a different direction. I kept pouring into broken vessels that weren't meant to contain the blessings of the next season I was walking into. New wine in an old wineskin. I kept believing that my effort could overcome their resistance. But trying to change people is like trying to walk up an escalator that's going down—you'll wear yourself out just to go nowhere.

People will be who they choose to be, and my job is to love them, not fix them. And I didn't realize I was trying to fix something in myself by trying to change something in them.

There are two types of wisdom that can help lead you to a conclusion like this:

The first is godly wisdom, which is a gift that is freely given if we seek it from God. We don't necessarily have to go through a situation to get this, but seek God's council.

The second is experiential wisdom, which comes after the emotional charge of an experience is gone, after the resentment fades, after the disappointment dissolves. Then you can see it clearly without the pain attached while the truth, to be paired with Scripture, remains.

Another big lesson I learned is this: success without God is failure in disguise. All those months of massive revenue? They were actually months of spiritual poverty. I was rich in the wrong currency, wealthy in things that wouldn't transfer to eternity, and running my head into a wall.

The wisdom is clear now: Any success that separates you from God is actually a sophisticated form of failure, designed to give you the appearance of success but leaving you without the fulfillment of alignment. Any victory that inflates your ego rather than your gratitude is actually a defeat.

And perhaps the hardest lesson: Human love, no matter how pure, cannot fill a God-shaped void. The love I've felt in the past few years is more than I'd ever experienced from another human. But even the deepest human love is only meant to reflect back to you an image of the love that the Creator has for you. True love shows up as a graceful mirror designed to point you home.

Only God's love is enough. Only his love never changes. Only his love never fails. Only his love can bear the full weight of your need without breaking.

The Valley of Transformation

Surrender is the first key to seeing things the way that God does. That wisdom that's left over after the emotion burns away? That's how God sees things. It's the truth from a higher lens. The objective reality is not imposed upon by your feelings or filtered through your fears. It's reality as it actually is, not as you wish it was.

Your first step to gaining sight is trusting that he can see something you don't. That his perspective is perfect, while yours is partial. That his wisdom is complete, while yours is fractured. You have to let go of your own sight and surrender to the experience in front of you in this present moment.

This means being completely and fully with the emotion, all the way through. Not checking out when it gets uncomfortable. Not reaching for your phone when the silence gets too loud. Not creating drama to avoid the deeper pain. Just sitting in it. Marinating in it. Letting it have its way with you until it's done.

Allow him to take you through the valley of the shadow of death. And yes, it will feel like death. Your ego will scream, your flesh will revolt, and everything in you will want to run.

But you can fear no evil because he is with you. You will find light on the other side (Ps. 23:4).

You have to sit in the feelings—really sit in them. Not just acknowledge them intellectually but feel them in your bones and let them move through you, letting yourself be purified as they come to the surface. Sit in the pain until it teaches you what it came to teach. Sit in the confusion until clarity emerges. Sit in the loss until you discover what remains.

But the most important thing to remember as you go through this is to trust in God's promises, which are timeless and will never change. As you read the Bible and pray, lean on God as the guide in the journey, the shepherd who knows what you feel and will remain faithful to you.

Wrestling with Angels

Wrestling with what is going on inside of you is one of the stepping-stones to deep, lasting transformation. Like Jacob wrestling with the angel, don't let go until you get your blessing. Even if it leaves you limping. Even if it changes how you walk forever. The blessing is worth the breaking, and you will receive a new name, a new identity on the other side of it.

We see in Genesis 32:24–26 NIV: "Jacob was left alone, and a man wrestled with him till daybreak. When the man saw that he could not overpower him, he touched the socket of Jacob's hip so that his hip was wrenched as he wrestled with the man. Then the man said, 'Let me go, for it is daybreak.' But Jacob replied, 'I will not let you go unless you bless me.'"

That's surrender—wrestling with God until he blesses you. Not letting go of him, even when it hurts. Not giving up, even when you're losing. Holding on with everything you have to your Father until he changes your name, your nature, and your destiny while trusting that he is sovereign and wants what's best for you.

I wrestled with God through sleepless nights, in tear-soaked prayers, and through arguments where I told him exactly how I felt about his plan. There were moments of rage where I accused him of cruelty and seasons of silence where he felt a million miles away.

Yet throughout all of that, I still held onto hope. Hope that his love was true, while doing my best to choose to believe that it was.

God doesn't hate your doubt.

In fact, he welcomes it and wants to help you overcome it. Doubt doesn't prevent faith; fear does. Doubt can still be felt while walking out the path. Even when all things around you say that you're losing, you may doubt that success is on the other side, but you can choose to walk faithfully through it.

Growing up wrestling for most of my life, I didn't realize the significance of it, and there was a deep lesson in it. My dad raised me to be a wrestler. I watched home videos of him wrestling with me as a baby, letting me feel like I was winning. He could've easily killed me if he wanted to. But by wrestling with him, a giant, I gained confidence and learned who I was.

God does the same thing with us. He is always taking it easy on us when we wrestle with him . . . he's God. The beauty of the wrestling match with him is that we get to find out who we are when it's all said and done. Learn to embrace the wrestling. It's not designed to punish you, but to build your fortitude.

We're all warriors when we choose to realize it, and it's not necessarily about winning the match.

It's about who you become in the process.

Daily Bread in the Desert

When the Israelites were in the wilderness, every single day, they were waiting on God to get them through. To give them their daily bread, their daily manna, just so they could survive another day (Exod. 16).

But notice something—God didn't give them a week's worth of manna. He didn't give them a month's supply. He gave them exactly what they needed for that day. Why? Because he wanted them dependent on *him*. He wanted them to be trusting. He wanted them looking up every single morning.

It wasn't just about surviving. It was surviving while knowing there was hope because they had God at the helm. God was guiding them forward, and it wasn't by their own efforts. They couldn't hunt their way out. They couldn't farm their way out. They couldn't strategize their way out. They had to trust their way through, or they would die.

Unfortunately, they were extremely stubborn and did just that, over and over. But some people eventually made it!

I'm still in a wilderness period now. Still walking through the desert. Still learning to depend on daily bread rather than stored grain while learning my gifts and calling. But the daily bread has been different than I expected, and each time I take a bite, I ingest a bit more clarity.

It's been reading the Bible first thing in the morning when my flesh wants to check my phone, and battling the tendency to want to revert. It's been praying when I want to plan. It's been making sure I'm not overcommitting myself when everything in me wants to sprint. It's been choosing God's presence over the presence of people when my heart gets confused about which one it needs more.

These simple things keep me going when everything feels uncertain. They're not sexy. They're not impressive. They aren't for Instagram. But they're sustaining me in a way that all my previous successes never could.

The manna is different in this season. Sometimes it's a verse that hits just right. Sometimes it's a moment of peace in the chaos or a new insight. Sometimes it's the strength to say no to an opportunity that would pull me back into old patterns. Sometimes it's the grace to forgive myself when I fail.

But it always comes. Every morning. Just enough for that day. Not enough to stockpile. Not enough to feel secure in my own provision. Just enough to remind me who my Provider is.

The Armor That Becomes a Prison

You have to be willing to lay down your armor. All that protection you've built up over the years and all those defense mechanisms that kept you safe but also kept you isolated. The very things that helped you survive are now preventing you from thriving.

For me, that armor was competence. Control. Charm. The ability to figure anything out. The capacity to push through any obstacle. The skill to make money out of thin air. The talent to make people love me. It's hilarious to think how I thought any of this was me and not God. That's the trap!

These weren't bad things; they were gifts. But I'd turned them into gods instead of realizing whom they came from. I'd made them my identity. And what were meant to be tools had become my prison.

Lay down your pride. It's too heavy anyway. You weren't meant to carry the weight of always being right, always being strong, and always being in control. That armor is crushing you, not protecting you.

Don't fight reality. Accept it. And through accepting reality, you can now gain the power of choice.

When you stop fighting what is, you can finally see what could be and who you truly are. When you stop resisting the present, you can finally create a different future. When you stop demanding that life meet your expectations, you can finally receive what life is trying to give you.

You can choose what is in front of you instead of being a victim to it. You become a victor through surrender, not despite it. You can have power—real power, lasting power, divine power—through God's power, which is bestowed upon you when you surrender to his will.

Here's what nobody tells you about surrender: It's not weakness. It's the ultimate power move. It's recognizing that your little kingdom is nothing compared to his eternal kingdom. It's trading your temporary control for his eternal sovereignty and exchanging your limited strength for his unlimited power.

I hated the word *surrender* because I associated it with the idea of losing or being captured by the enemy, but when I heard one of my favorite speakers, Myron Golden, refer to it as *yielding*, that's when the definition of it changed.

I yield my plan for God's. I yield my control of how things should be in my mind to how things should be in his: "But he said to me, 'My grace is sufficient for you, for my power is made perfect in weakness.' Therefore I will boast all the more gladly about my weaknesses, so that Christ's power may rest on me" (2 Cor. 12:9 NIV).

When I finally started to let go—really let go—of my business, my control, my plans, my relationship idolatry, something strange happened. Peace. Not the peace of resignation but the peace of alignment. Not the peace of giving up but the peace of giving over.

The business didn't die. It transformed. The relationship didn't end. It evolved. The vision didn't disappear. It clarified. Everything I thought I was losing by surrendering, I actually gained back in a purified form.

But I had to die first. The old me. The controlling me. The self-reliant me. The half-in-half-out me. The me who worshiped success and romance more than the God who gave them. That version had to be crucified with all his dreams and demands and delusions. Don't get me wrong; those things can still make an appearance, but now there's awareness it's easier to diminish their power.

Thank you, Jesus, for the grace, patience, and mercy you give as we walk the paths in front of us as your students.

What emerged from that death wasn't a weaker version of me. It was a submitted version of me. A version that could finally see clearly because he wasn't looking through the lens of his own agenda. A version that could finally hear clearly because he wasn't deafened by his own demands.

This is the pattern of the kingdom: death, then resurrection. Surrender, then power. Letting go, then receiving. You can't skip the death part. You can't fast-forward through the surrender. You can't bypass letting go. John 12:24 NIV states, "Very truly I tell you, unless a kernel of wheat falls to the ground and dies, it remains only a single seed. But if it dies, it produces many seeds."

I was a single seed, trying to be fruitful while refusing to fall into the ground. Refusing to be buried. Refusing to die. So I remained alone, no matter how much success I achieved or how deeply I was loved.

But when God finally broke through my resistance and planted me in the dark soil of surrender, something miraculous began to happen. The hard shell of my self-reliance began to crack. The roots of real faith began to grow. The fruit of the Spirit began to emerge.

I found love that wasn't dependent on being loved back and joy that wasn't tied to circumstances. Peace that wasn't contingent on control. Patience that wasn't forced but flowed. Kindness that wasn't calculated but natural. Goodness that wasn't performed but genuine. Faithfulness that wasn't grudging but glad. Gentleness that wasn't weakness but strength under control. Self-control that wasn't white-knuckling but Spirit-empowered.

For us to exhibit the fruits, we first have to be willing to be planted.

The Ongoing Journey

Surrender is the journey of life itself. It's not a onetime event but a daily practice. Every morning, I wake up and have to choose to surrender again. Every decision requires me to ask, "Am I doing things from my will or his?" Every opportunity demands that I evaluate: "Is God in this?"

Some days, I nail it. Some days, I've failed spectacularly. Some days, I catch myself making feelings my god again and have to repent. Some days, I catch myself obsessing over business metrics instead of kingdom metrics and have to reset.

But each day, I'm learning to see more clearly and perceive reality through his eyes rather than mine. To trust his perspective over my panic. To value what he values instead of what impresses people. And that's what we're really here to do, which all happens naturally as we learn to love God more fully.

The gift of vision—the ability to see life through the eyes of God—only comes to those who are willing to close their own eyes first. You have to choose whether you see things your way, or his way. You can perceive both, but you can only truly receive one.

And that comes down to surrender.

It's choosing his strength in your weakness, his wisdom in your confusion, and his plan in your chaos. You have to desire his love as your foundation instead of human affection, which will increase the more you think about all of the things he's done for you. His approval needs to be your validation instead of success metrics.

It's dying daily to the version of you that wants to be God so that the version of you made in God's image can finally live.

The Vision That Comes After Death

Now that you've started to learn how your vision can open up through surrender, how letting go allows you to finally see, we're going to talk about how to restore our perception of God. Because once you surrender your vision, you need to learn to see God as he truly is, not as your pain has painted him. Not as your parents represented him. Not as your failures have framed him.

And in that process of seeing him clearly, you'll discover who you really are. Your true identity is hidden in him. And you can only find it when you stop looking in the mirror and start looking at the throne.

You can only understand your worth when you understand the price he paid. You can only grasp your purpose when you grasp his plan. You can only see yourself clearly when you see him accurately.

The journey from blindness to sight always passes through the valley of surrender. There's no shortcut. No bypass. No express lane for the spiritually elite. Everyone who wants to see as God sees must first let go of how they see.

And that letting go? It's the doorway to everything you've been searching for.

Chapter 3 Implementation: Week 4

Teaching Point

That self-reliance that got you this far? It's now the very thing keeping you blind—because you can't receive with clenched fists. True vision comes when you let go of controlling and discovering that yielding to God brings true victory.

Mindset Shift

From "God should bless *my* plans" to "I die to my way to help fulfill his."

Prayer

"God, I confess I've been asking you to bless my plans for [fill in the blank] years instead of surrendering to yours. I've made success my god and her love my religion. I've been worshiping created things instead of my Creator. I repent. Help me let go of control. Show me where I'm still holding on. I don't know what I'm doing, and I need your help. Take what needs to be taken. Prune what needs to be pruned. I surrender my business, my relationship, my plans, my way. Help me worship you alone. Teach me that your love never changes like human love does. You *are* love, and that's enough. Give me daily bread for this wilderness. I die to my way so I can live in yours. In Jesus's name, amen."

Scriptures to Meditate On

- "I am the vine; you are the branches. Whoever abides in me and I in him, he it is that bears much fruit, for apart from me you can do nothing" (John 15:5 ESV).
- "You shall have no other gods before me" (Exod. 20:3 NIV).

- "God is love" (1 John 4:8 NIV).
- "Unless a kernel of wheat falls to the ground and dies, it remains only a single seed. But if it dies, it produces many seeds" (John 12:24 NIV).

Action Steps

1. **Double idol inventory.** Make two columns. Column 1: List everything you've made more important than God (success, money, achievement). Column 2: List every person whose approval or love you've valued more than God's. Circle your biggest idol in each column. Write a breakup letter to each idol (for the spirit of it), explaining why you can no longer worship it. Interact with it differently now.

2. **The life timeline.** Draw a timeline of your life. Mark every major success you achieved through self-reliance. Next to each one, write: "God blessed my effort" or "I thought it was just me." Notice the pattern. At the bottom, write: "For __ years, I asked God to bless *my* plans and thought I was doing it alone. Today I surrender to *his* plans."

3. **Daily reality check.** Each morning before you check your phone, bank account, or text anyone, get on your knees and say, "God, you are love. Your love never changes. Help me not make any person or thing my god today. I surrender." Then read 1 John 4:8 and sit in silence for five minutes, letting his unchanging love fill you before you seek it anywhere else.

CHAPTER 4 SEEING GOD AS HE TRULY IS

If you're like me, it took you a while to actually see who God really was. Maybe you're one of the people who grew up knowing Jesus since you were young, but that was not the case for me. In fact, I was viewing him wrong my entire life.

For many of those years, I knew a lot about God. I could tell you theological concepts. Quote spiritual principles. Discuss the nature of consciousness and Source energy. But I didn't know him. He was conceptual—a "Source" we come from that didn't have much personality. An energy field. A universal consciousness. Everything except a person I could actually relate to.

I couldn't see him as he truly is because I was looking through lenses purely dictated by my own experiences. I still felt love for him, but not the same type of love I do now. I didn't connect the idea of Jesus and Source together internally, so I wasn't actually relating with anyone, just a thing and myself. That leads to thinking, "I am God," which is not the truth at all.

So how do we fix our perception of God in the first place?

The Projection Problem

What I've talked about before is how our relationship with our parents can put a projection onto God that may or may not be true. Our parents' job is to show us who God is through their character, through the way they lead us, as much as they possibly can. It's never going to be perfect because they're human, but it's their job to point us to God and help us see his love.

Depending on how you grew up, maybe you had a dad who was able to relate with you only through performance. Maybe it was only through work. Maybe it felt like you weren't enough at times. Maybe it felt like he was distant. Maybe it felt like he was overbearing.

Whatever it is, there's a high, high chance you've projected that onto God. We don't always see God as he is. We tend to see him through the stories we've told ourselves.

We must first look at what views of God have come from our relationship with our dad. Or even if you didn't have a dad—the lack of a dad can translate into a lack of God in your life. The absence itself becomes the projection that can lead to striving and more.

I thought for most of my life that God was just this boss in the sky. Transactional. Performance-based. He didn't want a relationship with me—he just wanted results. He was an authority I had to be scared of, not a Father I could run to.

And because I was scared of him, I actually secretly resented and hated God, which made me want to rebel. Can you relate to that? That hidden resentment toward someone you're supposed to love?

Because I secretly resented and hated him, but also didn't want to disappoint him, I would do things to try and please him while being spiteful at the same time. My heart wanted to do the opposite of what he said. I was the spiritual equivalent of a teenager—outwardly compliant, inwardly defiant and annoying.

This made me a great entrepreneur. It made me very self-reliant. I was able to find my own way. I became resourceful. I generated skills and all types of stuff that helped me create a life on my own terms. But I was being rebellious unconsciously. Not coming to the fact that even though I said I loved God, I didn't actually love him with all my heart.

It was only as much as I would allow myself to. Because I thought fully being open and loving with him would have me taken advantage of or manipulated somehow. I didn't see that submission to him was actually the way to find the love I was truly looking for.

The Mirror of Relationships

I had to take some time to look at myself, to look at my own relationships, and to ask myself hard questions. Why did I struggle in relationships with women? Why does my relationship with my parents feel frustrating? Why do my friendships not feel that consistent all the time?

I had to look at these relationships around me and see the common denominator in all of them. Oh. It was me. Glorious.

Because I saw that I was the common denominator, that meant there was something I was doing or believing that was contributing to the dysfunction. My view of God was bleeding into every human relationship I had.

There was something I believed that led to this reality in front of me. I had to see these beliefs inside myself. Encounter them. Go back into my past and ask where they were formed. I had to see if they were actually true.

Like the belief of "They weren't there for me" leading to my believing that God wasn't there for me, I had to actually look back at my life and see all the times he was. Once I had awareness that this belief was untrue, I could choose to consciously change it and look for evidence in my environment of how he has been there for me.

This is rewriting the story we have about reality so we don't see what we think is true, but what is actually the truth.

The Worldwide Wild-Goose Chase

The funny thing is, I was doing all of this without the Bible. The Bible makes life so much simpler (not easier—big difference), even though the flesh hates it. But I went to every part of the freaking world. I left this dimension while doing plant medicine. I jumped out of planes. I did all types of things to try and discover God and find the truth. Everything other than open the Bible. All of it left me empty and feeling like Solomon in Ecclesiastes as he was on his "meaningless" journey to figure out the purpose of life.

I literally climbed to the top of Mount Kilimanjaro. Picture this: There I was, 19,341 feet above sea level, standing on the roof of Africa. I'd spent days climbing, altitude sickness threatening to take me down, all because I thought transcendence was waiting at the summit. I was hoping to find answers up there. Some divine revelation in the thin air where earth meets heaven.

What I found instead was a humbling realization of how insignificant I am in the scheme of things. I was this tiny speck on the world's tallest freestanding mountain, and it's just a pimple on the earth. Standing there, gasping for breath, I couldn't escape how small I was.

I look back now, and it makes me realize how much God loves us— that he sees how small we are and still cares about every detail of our lives more than anything else.

I tried psylocibin and ayahuasca. Now I want to be crystal clear here—nobody should do this, and I'm not suggesting it. I left that life behind, and it's not necessary. But my experience, which I'd be a fool to pretend didn't happen and hide, as dangerous and misguided as it was, ended up being used by God to lead me deeper to Jesus.

During one of the two aya ceremonies, I had a vision of him. I experienced a journey of dying and being resurrected, as if I were on a cross. It sounds crazy—I know it sounds crazy—but that's what I experienced. The physical agony. The spiritual abandonment. The moment of death. Then resurrection. It helped me to understand what Jesus went through and to empathize with him. My intent for that night was to understand Jesus after all.

After that time away, I came back home with an insatiable hunger for the Word and didn't need to do plant medicine again. God has a way of using our rebellion to reveal his redemption.

I destroyed my ego in these ceremonies. It felt like my "self" had disintegrated. It was an ego death and more, the final one being the one when I actually experienced death. When I came back, I looked at people around me, and they were me. They were still "them," but I was viewing them from essence and soul, so I was seeing theirs. We were one. So was everything around me. I could see the connecting life behind everything that made things be.

I thought it was me connecting and guiding us. But it was God.

I came home from that final ceremony convinced that I was God, not realizing that I'm just a fractal of God's nature, just like a son is a fractal of their father's essence. Linked to him, but not the entire thing. We're children of his.

I can't put it into words other than that, but I really want to iterate—I left that life behind. Don't do it. It's not necessary. God can reveal himself without you poisoning yourself trying to find him.

I know there will be people tweaking out, screaming to themselves, "Blasphemy! Demon!" Listen, if sharing my salvation story makes me a demon, then I don't know what to tell you other than to take it to Jesus. He didn't water the truth down, he stood as it.

Building Monuments to Find Him

I built things so he would be proud of me. Successful businesses. Impressive achievements. Thinking if I just accomplished enough, he'd finally show up and validate me. I tried to find him in relationships, thinking that if I just found the right person who loved me enough, I'd finally feel his love through them. All of this was happening subconsciously; I had no idea what I was doing.

I tried to find him everywhere other than where he's already spoken—which is the Bible. Because the thing about humanity is that we tend to like complexity more than simplicity. We think things have to be a lot harder than they actually are. We want the treasure hunt, the secret knowledge, the hidden path that only the spiritually elite can find. Yes, he conceals a matter. But it's usually concealed in plain sight.

God is simple and honest and truthful. Most things are way simpler than we can comprehend. We think there's some trap to it if we listen to what he's saying. This is the same exact thing that happened in the Garden of Eden. We think he's withholding something.

But he is the truth itself. Not *a* truth. Not *containing* truth. He *is* truth. There's nobody and nothing else to trust.

The Character Without the Person

I discovered different aspects of God through my life experiences. I experienced him as a Redeemer when he pulled me out of dark places. As someone who gave endurance when I pushed through impossible challenges. I experienced him when I had confidence standing in front of crowds. These experiences came through exploring the world, building my business, and starting to heal from shame and trauma.

But I didn't know his real identity. I only knew aspects of his character.

Through only knowing aspects of his character, we can't fully know who he is. Because we don't know who it is that's carrying that character. It's like knowing someone is kind, generous, and wise, but never knowing their name or face. You can't have a relationship with attributes. You need a person who carries them.

It wasn't until I opened the Bible that I saw that Jesus was the one who had all these elements of character, but he also had an identity. Through that identity, I could relate to him—because he was a man and not just a concept.

I used to relate to God as only a concept. I thought he was just "Source" alone. But I didn't realize he also came as a man. I didn't want to admit it.

Because part of me had a belief that said, "I don't want a man to have authority over me. I don't trust a man to have authority over me because he'll mislead me and want me to be in pain and hurt."

So many emotions came through different experiences in my life. Growing up. Going through school. Life itself put these beliefs in my head that made me want to reject that authority. Do you feel that resistance too? That part of you that bristles at the idea of submitting to anyone, even God?

I had to look at myself and see where I wasn't able to come to the idea of having a man over me who is an authority. I had to learn how to let that go by gently submitting myself to the promises, principles, and things that are spoken in the Bible.

Throughout the journey of doing that, I discovered that my life did start to feel more aligned. I started to feel more peace. I felt more . . . myself. The more I started to find myself through the Bible, the more I found God in the process.

I started to realize that the more he covered me, the less I had to cover myself. This helped me see him as a God who is truly trustworthy and reduce my self-preservation in the process.

The Baptizer Who Wasn't Baptized

Even at the end of 2024, he was using me to baptize people. Which made zero sense.

One of my older brothers—not by blood but by love and relationship—coached me and helped me through a lot of dark periods. He came to me to baptize him. The same day, one of my friends who's like a little bro to me, also came to me, wanting to be baptized after I told him I was going to drive across the state to do so. So I drove to West Palm Beach from Tampa, Florida—four hours—to go baptize these two guys.

All I could ask was "Why me?" I mean, I was baptized spiritually when I had a spiritual awakening in college as I experienced oneness. My life transformed after that—I just didn't have the right name or terms for it at the time. I was just living my life. But I hadn't been water baptized in the traditional sense. I had to look up how to baptize someone on Google and check that I could. It confirmed that I could because it was in Jesus's name, not mine, and I considered myself a believer.

It felt like a meme, but I obviously couldn't turn it down. What else would I do on a Saturday? I couldn't think of anything more honorable than helping someone publicly declare their faith.

A few months later, another friend who was Muslim, after a bunch of our conversations and him having a very humbling experience in his life, came to me, wanting to be baptized. I was apparently showing the character of Christ in how we related, and he hadn't experienced the level of forgiveness I was giving him, empowered by the Holy Spirit. For me, it felt normal, and I justified it with "It's just the right thing to do."

Three friends I baptized, all different backgrounds, a few months apart. It all came down to this: God uses imperfect people to pour out his perfect love.

These men came to me to baptize them. And I'm like, "God, why are you having me do this? I'm not even a minister. I'm not any of this. I'm just a guy." But God apparently saw something different.

It was crazy that one was my coach who had helped me through so much, and another led the ayahuasca retreat—two people who had been "spiritual authorities" in my life were now coming to me. I just felt humbled and thankful. But I had to humble myself quickly again and realize that it wasn't even about me!

The Relentless Love

Through these acts of love and honor, God kept honoring me when I was dishonoring him. In my speech, my actions, my character, even when I was being an idiot—he kept showing me love.

I wondered, "Why is God so kind? What is he doing?" It didn't make any sense to me.

The consistency of his love over time softened my heart. All I could think was, "Wow, he is so loving, and I don't deserve any of this."

But here's where I messed up. I thought he was going to be always loving in the sense that I would never have to face repercussions for my actions. That his love meant no consequences. That grace meant no discipline. That was not the case.

I still faced a lot of pain. I still had to face the circumstances and consequences of my actions over time. But even when I had to face that pain, even when I had to face grief, he was there in it with me. I started to see it as disciplinary love instead of punishment.

The Night Everything Changed

One of the biggest revelations came through encountering the relationship with lust I had in myself—one of the generational family curses I've had to go to war with. He pulled it out of me. Of course, just like anyone, I still feel temptations in life, but this was different.

I remember having one of the worst nights of my life ever. I was driving to go do a sauna and cold plunge to reset my nervous system and body after a hard week relationship-wise. I remember saying a prayer after watching a video that said to have Jesus do a deliverance on you.

So I prayed out loud in the name of Jesus to have him deliver me from the spirit of lust I was dealing with, from the spirit of pornography, from the spirit of pride, from the spirit of all types of things that were inside me since I was young that needed to go.

Later that night, I got home and just burst into tears, listening to worship music. The music was speaking to my soul, and I was feeling it deep in my heart. Every note brought tears and deep grief. I was in a relationship separation and regretting a lot of what I had done, with a mix of anger and resentment for feeling abandoned, and abandoning myself. It was an emotional roller coaster.

Out of nowhere, I just felt this urge to puke. I went to the bathroom, bent over the toilet, and started puking. But nothing physical was coming out. Yet it was the deepest throw-up I've ever felt in my life.

I could feel energy coming out of my body, in the form of grief removing itself. The energy leaving was like heavy, dense grief coming up slowly from the gut and pouring out invisibly into the toilet. It felt like an alien parasite climbing out of me.

That night, Jesus pulled something out of me. He pulled these feelings, this grief, this deep pain, guilt, and shame out from my soul. He was cleansing me.

I knew for a fact it was him. I knew it was him because nothing else made sense.

After all of that, my girlfriend showed up out of nowhere when I was praying to Jesus for help, begging him on my knees, also wanting to see her. The timing was not coincidental but divinely orchestrated.

She prayed over me to release shame, even while not wanting to see me.

I knew that Jesus had given me mercy and grace in that moment. I felt like lust didn't have the same stronghold as it did before.

His grace frees us from who we've been, while showing us who we are in his eyes at the same time. The love I felt from him when I called on his name—and him answering it, even with the shame I was experiencing—allowed me to see what I was doing. I immediately broke down in tears and repentance.

It was only through seeing his heart as I drew closer to him that I knew he was real. But the catalyst was when he delivered me from the deep sexual shame and trauma that were making me live as if I were unworthy, and had haunted me my whole life.

Every Path Led to Him

Even when I did ayahuasca, my final night when I got casually and absolutely destroyed by a panther and the spirit of death (a superlong story), I ended up coming to a full realization of Jesus when I experienced firsthand a moment that was like being crucified. What it meant to die for those around you. Seeing that he was the purpose for everything. Again, I'm not promoting this.

Don't read that from the lens of "Does that guy really think he can compare himself to Jesus?" No, obviously not. I understood his heart behind the action, though.

I also saw how we, beings in a 3-D world, can only know someone or something else if we relate to it. Relationships not only tell us who someone is, but also who we are. How would we relate to the infinite if the infinite remained infinite and we remained finite?

We couldn't. Jesus had to come to be finite for a moment in time to reconcile us to eternal communion. He is the Lens for us to see the eternal in the finite. He is the Message and the Messenger at the same time. He's the whole point.

Every experience I went through pointed me back to Jesus. Not always directly, but in a way that I kept seeing how what I was doing wasn't the full truth, yet it had some aspect or characteristic of him within it. Most faiths focus on one single aspect of God without the full revelation of him, that's why it can feel true when you're in it but lacks completeness.

Every single moment was used to point me back to him. I could not escape him, no matter what I did. No matter what religion I explored. No matter what path I stormed to find the answer.

Buddhism taught me meditation and expanded my awareness, which helped me gain more of a mental understanding of him. But it felt incomplete. It was also empty and self-focused.

Hinduism had elements in the Bhagavad Gita that were similar to biblical insights and stories, but they were different. It felt off because there were so many gods. Too many options. Too much confusion. Not real and relatable, and still not as "real" in feel as following Christ.

Islam made me realize how Jesus and the Bible did not feel as performative or works-based in comparison. Five prayers a day. Constant striving. Never knowing if you've done enough.

Religious Judaism, which I grew up in, is similar. Very surface level and hardheaded, with more of a worship of the label than the true incarnation of God, the Messiah whom everyone was waiting for.

These paths didn't necessarily lead me to Christ, but they narrowed down my options to him after I realized that they all felt like they were missing the thing my soul was craving. I just didn't know what that was.

Now I look back, and I can't go back. Those other religions are like worshiping an aspect of God's design but not God in his totality. I cannot go back to seeing things in those ways because I have experienced the answer, which is Jesus. It would be like worshiping his arm.

Everything pointed me back to him. The other paths all referenced him in some way. Yet Jesus was the only one who said, "I am the way and the truth and the life. No one comes to the Father except through me" (John 14:6 NIV).

I had to finally humble myself and realize that no matter where I go, I end up back at Jesus. So maybe it's something worth exploring.

The Difference Between Seeing Things and Seeing Him

As I read the Bible and experienced God's grace and mercy, I felt a transformation of my heart. He started to make himself clearer. He was already answering prayers, but now I could *see* him answering prayers. That was the difference.

I started to actually see him moving around me because before, I was blind. I wasn't trying to see him moving around me. I just wanted to see the things moving. I didn't want to see him moving in the things.

You have to ask yourself: "Is my heart wanting to see him in the world around me and inside myself in all the circumstances I face? Or am I just wanting to see things change?"

There are two choices in pain. You either choose just relief, which is a change of your circumstance, or you choose repentance, which is a change of heart that seeks a relationship with the One who's creating and allowing all of the circumstances.

Relief changes your situation. Repentance changes you.

This is the difference. Repentance happens through allowing yourself to see his true character and to embrace it, reading the Bible as if it's written by Jesus himself, reading about how he already walked the earth, and seeing the people around you who have a relationship with him and the fruits of the Spirit they exemplify.

Seeing the nature of creation—how it's healing, rejuvenating, restoring—you see how all of it is linked back to him. I mean, the sun rises up from the dark every day! How are we missing this?

If you soften your heart enough—which is a choice—and you allow yourself to look for him and seek out the good in him instead of the bad without trying to prove yourself right . . . you will find that the bad is not from him. Bad is only in your circumstances, and it's simply a perception that's from Satan: "Every good and perfect gift is from above, coming down from the Father of the heavenly lights" (James 1:17 NIV). If you have your mind on the Lord, you can be grateful even through death, which is technically the worst mortal experience we can go through. But look how Jesus ended up after that one!

If you seek out God and you truly want to find him with all of your heart, with all your curiosity, with everything in your soul, he will make himself known, because as it's said in the Bible: "Come near to God and he will come near to you" (James 4:8 NIV).

The Bible really is the key to seeing God for who he is in Jesus. One, because the entire time you read it, the Old Testament is revealing his character and all of the miracles he's going to do in advance. But then Jesus comes into the New Testament, and he reflects all those elements of his character. He fulfills the prophetic things that he's doing in the Old Testament. He's being consistent with who he was, even if many people around him were still blind.

I was really confused for a lot of my life about what God thought about me. I thought I was a good person, but I knew there was stuff I had to clear out in myself. There were blocks and beliefs I had to remove, and it took identity deaths and hardship to get me to move.

I was doing a lot of that removal by my own will. I thought it was me controlling the whole thing. I thought I was God, and that he was just a sidekick to give my thoughts to every now and again. But his mercy and grace kept me alive long enough to find him. His patience outlasted my pride. His love was stronger than my rebellion.

All of these positive things about him helped me gain clarity of the negative things in me. The biggest ones of all were self-centeredness and self-preservation, which I still wrestle with, but just like anything, they can be overcome with reps and leaning on God.

The more you raise yourself up, the smaller he gets. The more you lower yourself, the more room there is in your life for his presence to be known. If you want more proximity to God, you must get out of your own way.

Seeing Yourself Through His Eyes

Now that you've found some steps to help you see God for who he truly is, now it's time for you to see yourself how God sees you.

Because here's the truth: You can't see yourself clearly until you see him clearly. Every distortion in how you view God creates a corresponding distortion in how you view yourself, and how you view reality.

Take the story of Samson and Delilah in Judges and connect the dots here. After multiple attempts by Delilah to take down Samson and his strength, with Samson being too much of an idiot to see them, she finally gets him to admit that if his hair is removed, then he will lose his power. She lulls him to sleep, just as sin and false beliefs do, and his hair is removed by a Philistine. She then cries out, "Samson! The Philistines have come to capture you!"

Side note: He ignored this red flag so many times. I write this and can't help but think, "Wow, this guy is so stupid." Yet I'd be a hypocrite if I acted like I haven't done this before to know how stupid it is.

Samson wakes up and realizes that the Lord has left him, and that he didn't see it as it was happening. What happens next is very important, and sums this up, so stay with me.

It says, "So the Philistines captured him and gouged out his eyes" (Judg. 16:21, paraphrased).

What does this mean? It means that since Samson was spiritually blind, physical reality eventually reflected it back to him with actual blindness. This is why we need to check our beliefs, especially the ones we can't see, or we will get lulled to sleep and stay blind.

If you see God as distant, you'll see yourself as abandoned. If you see him as angry, you'll see yourself as guilty. If you see him as transactional, you'll see yourself living in a performance. If you see him as a concept, you'll see yourself as an idea.

But when you see him as he truly is—a loving Father who sent his Son to die for you while you were still sinning, who pursues you relentlessly, who pulls the poison out of your soul, who uses you, even in your brokenness—then you can finally see yourself as you truly are.

Loved. Chosen. Redeemed. His.

In the next chapter, we'll talk about how reality is a mirror and how it's always showing you yourself. But first, you need to see the One who's holding the mirror.

Because until you see God as he truly is, you'll never see yourself as you truly are.

Chapter 4 Implementation: Week 5

Teaching Point

With your hands finally open, you can see who's been pursuing you all along—not necessarily who your parents modeled but the Father who runs toward prodigals. When you stop seeing God through your wound filters and start seeing Jesus, everything changes because Love himself is staring back.

Mindset Shift

From "God is distant Source energy" to "God is the Father who never left."

Prayer

"Jesus, I confess I've been seeing you through broken lenses—through my pain, my parents, my past. I've searched the whole world, looking for you everywhere except where you've already revealed yourself. Forgive me for making you a concept instead of a person, a Source instead of a Savior. Pull out of me whatever keeps me from seeing you clearly—the resentment, the fear, the pride, the lust. I call on your name like I'm drowning, because without you, I am. Show me who you really are. Show me your heart. I'm tired of knowing about you. I want to know you, as a Father. Come near to me as I come near to you. In Jesus's name, amen."

Scriptures to Meditate On

- "I am the way and the truth and the life. No one comes to the Father except through me" (John 14:6 NIV).
- "Come near to God and he will come near to you" (James 4:8 NIV).

- "Every good and perfect gift is from above, coming down from the Father of the heavenly lights" (James 1:17 NIV).

Action Steps

1. **Parent projection inventory.** Write down how you saw your earthly father (distant, demanding, absent, etcetera). Next to each trait, write how you've projected that onto God. Then find a scripture that shows God's true nature in that area. Example: "Dad was distant" → "God feels distant" → "I will never leave you nor forsake you" (Heb. 13:5 ESV).

2. **The seeking map.** Draw a map of everywhere you've looked for the essence of God without God (achievement, relationships, substances, religions, etcetera). At each location, write what you found instead. Then draw an arrow from every dead end pointing to the Bible. Open it today and read John 1. Jesus is the Word made flesh.

3. **The Deliverance Prayer.** If you're ready, pray out loud, with reverence, for Jesus to deliver you from whatever has you in bondage. Be specific. Name it. Then pay attention over the next days and weeks. Document what he removes and what he replaces it with. He doesn't leave you empty—he fills you with himself. He may even require you to go confront something. Listen to him and do whatever is needed.

CHAPTER 5 THE MIRROR OF HEAVEN

The biggest disease in all of humanity is that we don't realize who we are because we don't realize who God is.

And when we start to see ourselves how God sees us, then all of the problems in our life can change. Why is this? Because everything is an identity problem. Everything you have in your reality is based on what you do. And what you do is based on who you are.

If you change who you see yourself as, in belief and perception, you naturally end up becoming someone different. When you do this, you automatically end up doing what you need to do to have what you want to have as that person, because it stems from new identity.

Myron Golden talks about the concept of "be, do, have" over and over on his YouTube and other teaching outlets, which is the creative process contained within Genesis and how God creates the heavens and the earth.[2] It's really crazy to think about if you take the time to do so.

"I can change what my brain has inside of it and everything around me will change?"

Yes, exactly. That's why . . .

We have to see ourselves how God sees us to experience the life that's truly meant for us. And if God is the only One who is truly good, as Jesus says, then maybe it's a good idea to listen to him.

The Mirror Principle

One of the things I've learned in my journey is a principle I call the mirror principle. This means seeing every single thing around you as a reflection of something going on within you—energetically, mentally, emotionally, spiritually, or even physically.

Think about this: How many times in your life have you noticed one problem showing up everywhere? Whether it's in relationships, your business, your job, or just in your body. Then you notice you're dealing with the same type of problem in some other area of your life as well. You keep experiencing the same patterns over and over, yet somehow don't realize that you may be the common denominator.

Maybe you went through a long string of relationships where you didn't know why you kept encountering the same type of people and having the same problems. Maybe you had a win at work, only to watch everything falling apart right after, multiple times.

Wherever you go, the problems go with you. So look at whom the problems are attached to. This means there's something in you that

---

[2] Myron Golden in David Shands and Donni Wiggins, "The 3 Stages of Success: Be, Do, Have – Episode # 218 w/ Myron Golden," *Social Proof Podcast,* February 7, 2022.

has to be faced or changed. Don't do it out of self-judgment, but simply observe. This is compassionate, radical self-responsibility.

Yes, there can also be spiritual warfare. There are many times that is true and you want to weaponize your prayers. But what I've found in my time on this Earth is that we give demons and the enemy way more credit than they deserve. Sometimes we can just be bathing ourselves in a victim mentality, forgetting that God gave us authority to rule. When we submit to that truth and start viewing things as if we're directly responsible for them in some way, it may feel tough, but it means that we had the power to make it happen in some sense. We aren't just helpless bugs.

Therefore, we have the power to undo it as well, because we have the power of God on our side. When you take on a victor mentality instead of a victim mentality, you get the One who had the final victory as a by-product. See your reality as if God entrusted you with it, not as if he just put you here to float around.

For me, this negative mindset showed up everywhere. In most of my relationships—friendships, business, romantic attachments—I'd attract people whom I would get frustrated with. People who wouldn't meet my standards. I'd devalue them constantly, finding fault, getting annoyed at their limitations. I couldn't see that I was setting the astronomically high standards so that they would fail.

Then one day, it hit me like a brick to the face. I was devaluing myself as I devalued them. I was attracting people who reflected my feelings of inner unworthiness back to me, because I wouldn't let them go when I realized they weren't aligned with where I was going. They were my mirrors, showing me exactly what I thought of myself. They were pointing me back to my own inner frustration with myself and life, because under the surface, I didn't think I was worthy of a life that flowed instead of forced.

This inner frustration with myself affected everything around me. I saw it clearly in my business. As I became more annoyed and frustrated, my team would feel stressed out. The energy I brought to meetings would determine the energy of the entire room. When I was scattered, they were scattered. When I was harsh, they became defensive or hid from speaking up. When I was unclear, they were confused.

I had to start seeing that the people I was leading were reflecting my blocks back to me. I wasn't taking full responsibility for my emotions. I was blaming things around me for what was actually my internal state being projected outward, and I was completely blind to it.

I was like the Pharisees, trying to control things so I would feel good about myself.

Once we see in ourselves what this block is, what needs to be changed, then we can actually see that things outside of us are reflections of that. We can choose to do something else inside of us, which leads to a different external result.

But here's the caveat . . . we have to want to see it.

The Difference Between Suffering and Stagnation

Suffering to get to a goal is part of the journey. But that's purposeful suffering. Most people, myself included, have been stuck in suffering for the sake of suffering, keeping ourselves there. That happens when you're experiencing constant pain and struggle for no reason, and it's not moving in a positive direction.

If you're constantly staying stuck, that means it's an area of your life that God is not living in fully. You're most likely keeping him out of it to hold on to your own way, or who you think "you" are. God is abundant and free, and when we let Christ into a certain area of our life, we experience that freedom. If you're not experiencing that internal freedom, then you're not fully living in the truth of who you are.

Look at the promises God has said over you versus what you're experiencing. There are countless ones in the Bible. You're "more than conquerors through him who loved us" (Rom. 8:37 NIV). You're someone of honor and valor, like when God called Gideon a "mighty warrior" while he was hiding in a winepress (Judg. 6:12).

I experienced that last one personally, going up to the altar one night when I was in a rough season and seeking Jesus's presence. Someone came up behind me and put their hands on me while saying, "You are a mighty man of honor and valor." I knew God was using them to speak life into who he saw me as, not who I saw myself as. Not what my circumstances said about me.

Look at Moses. He's another great example of a doubter whom God used for amazing purposes. Moses doubted himself, had a speech impediment, and murdered someone, yet God still sent him to fulfill a purpose. "Who am I that I should go to Pharaoh?" Moses asked. And God's response? "I will be with you" (Exod. 3:11–12 NIV).

Abraham didn't believe he could have a son at one hundred years old, yet God told him he would if he just had faith. And he became the father of nations (Gen. 17:5).

God doesn't view us based on who we are now. He views us based on who he designed us to become. He's seeing our present, our past, and our future, all collapsed into one point of meaning that defines who we are and the story we're here to walk out while we're alive.

It's up to us to agree with that, though, and disagree with what's false. We have to choose to let ourselves, and the old patterns of suffering attached to them, go. How?

Breaking False Agreements

Look at your life. Where is your language different from what God has said about you? Where are you making false agreements with the voice of doubt, with the voice of confusion in your head—which is also Satan and the strongholds that have been planted in you— telling you to remain in scarcity, to remain in lack, to remain stuck?

Because if you keep reinforcing those things in your head, whether you know it or not, you're agreeing to those things. And those agreements are what keep you stuck.

These agreements could have happened in the past. From a loss. From a traumatic event. Maybe even from something your parents told you when you were a kid. Maybe someone made fun of you in school and it made you doubt your own abilities.

You know how people say not to use God's name in vain? What if every time you said, "I am . . ." and followed it with anything not aligned with what God says about you, you were using his name in vain? How many times out of the day have you been saying God's name in vain? Too many to count. We don't even realize it.

Here is an example of an agreement I had made without realizing it.

I was in chorus with one of my friends in fourth grade after he convinced me to join. I actually loved singing, but I did it alone and when nobody could hear me. It felt natural, joyful, like something I was meant to do. Was it good? Not necessarily. But I was focused on the joy of just simply vibing as a kid.

Then a rumor spread around the school—or at least among the dudes in our grade—that I was into guys because I liked to sing, and it was only my friend and I singing among a crowd of girls at our fourth-grade chorus show. They started saying I was gay for wanting to be in chorus. The savagery of unfiltered childhood!

I was ten years old. And in that moment, I made an agreement: Singing makes me less of a man. It makes me like a woman or a guy who likes dudes. Satan was whispering to me, "Look how all the guys are watching you and you're up here with a bunch of girls. You're one of them."

I never wanted to sing again. For sixteen-ish years, I shut down that part of myself. It took me until I was about twenty-six years old to start actually singing with purpose again. And you know what prompted it? My girlfriend brought it up. She said she wanted to sing together, and she signed up for singing lessons. Something in me wanted to sing with her, to share that intimacy. But it also gave me a reason to let my voice come back to the surface and stop holding back.

When I finally opened my mouth to sing again, I didn't realize why I'd been so resistant for all those years until I thought back to that fourth-grade moment. A false agreement made by a nine-year-old boy had controlled a grown man for nearly two decades.

It felt freeing when I finally broke it, like reclaiming a piece of my soul I'd abandoned. I've been getting better ever since, finding more enjoyment in self-expression, in being myself authentically without worrying what anyone thinks about my masculinity.

That was made up. It was just not a real belief. It was a false agreement.

And you know what's funny? Those things that we have the most resistance to doing are the things that God usually calls us to the most.

I used to basically black out when giving speeches in school because of my fear of public speaking. I signed up to theater class in college to get over it. I was shaking every time I'd go in, but then the class went online during COVID-19 and became a voice-over class. I became the best. It made me realize I wasn't scared of being heard, but seen. That's when I went on TikTok, and that grew to six hundred thousand people in a couple of years. After that, I started hosting in-person retreats so I could be comfortable taking what I was sharing online into an in-person environment.

The same thing happened. I was nervous at the first one, but it ended up amazing. The second was even better.

Then, regarding singing, my music teacher (who follows Scientology) convinced me to do a talent show. I ended up rapping and singing a song I wrote from scratch about Jesus in front of more than three hundred people in a talent show inside of a Scientology building in Clearwater, Florida.

It was the most nerve-racking and freeing experience of my life. Now I'm hooked. I don't know what else there is to do that can be used to help me expose my voice beyond singing now, where my most authentic self has to come out and be seen. At this point, it's simply about more of what I've already done, in higher quantities, if God permits it. Either way, and no matter the stage, I feel like I conquered a Goliath. That's what I want for you.

So what's the lesson in this? When you lean into the fears, you overcome them. You become someone new.

Yes, spiritual warfare exists, and you want to pray it away. But if you're just praying to overcome doubt and not actually moving into it with faith, you're missing the point. You break false agreements by walking away from them, and toward the God who spoke into who he designed you to be.

Choosing God's Truth over Your History

You need to self-analyze—like we said before—and go back to your past. (Are you getting why I keep saying this over and over?)

Look at the agreements you've made that are false. Even if you don't know if they're false, look at them. They're usually in the areas where you experience the most friction. Put them next to God's Word and God's promises for your life. Ask yourself the following questions: "Am I more willing to trust what God has said about me, or am I willing to trust the same broken pattern that has kept me stuck my entire life? Am I more addicted to the pain, or am I more addicted to the promises God has said over my life? Do I believe I am a child of God? One who has been given authority? Or do I believe I'm a victim to my circumstances?"

These are choices you have to make. If you aren't going to do the work to make the right ones, though, I don't know how you would've ended up in this book, because clearly you are.

Yes, it will be hard. It will be hard to overcome these beliefs because you have to rewire your neural pathways. It's like the highways we talked about earlier. You're going to have to starve out the old highways by having awareness to remove attention from them and transfer that attention to a new highway that's being built up every day, every time you give energy and intention to it.

This is going to take conscious repetition, conscious work. That's why it's a daily battle. This is why we have to have a daily renewing of our minds, as Paul talked about in Romans 12:2. It's a constant thing we have to do. We have to make sure we stay aware and maintain our momentum because Satan wants to come in and derail us, to pull us into those past patterns as soon as he can so we forget who we are.

If you forget who you are, then thanks to the be-do-have formula we discussed earlier, you will then take the wrong actions and end up with a life that's hell. That's Satan's favorite hobby: being a devil.

The Orphan Spirit

God sees you as fruitful and abundant, because you're his kid. As he says in Genesis, "Be fruitful and multiply" (1:28 ESV). He's designed you to be fruitful. Yes, it has to do with expanding the human race, but he's designed you with the ability to multiply life. He put the ability to be fruitful inside you.

But here's yet another big choice. You choose whether you're going to be fruitful and multiply the pain, fear, and suffering—or whether you're going to be fruitful and multiply the blessings and abundance he has already bestowed upon you as his child. For those who think that we don't get to choose anything in life and it's all up to God, sit on that one. We choose his way, or we don't. That's proof we have a part to play in how this journey goes.

This all requires perspective shifting. It requires us to start seeing ourselves differently, to start noticing our thoughts and shifting our mindsets to match God's language rather than our own or Satan's voice that he planted inside us.

And this all starts from recognizing that you are a son or daughter of God. You have to actually desire that.

I had an orphan spirit my entire life. I didn't want to be a son, truly, because I felt there was too much pain attached, and I didn't have the full spiritual identity of a son from when I was young, even though my own dad was doing what he knew and thought was right. I had to earn a relationship with God by doing things, like partaking in the rituals on Hanukkah, Rosh Hashanah, Yom Kippur, Passover, and more. I felt that God's love for me could be taken away if I didn't do the right things, and the ritualistic relationship eventually led to me not caring. Praying was a foreign concept. I didn't see God as a Father, just as an idea, so I didn't really care. I learned self-confidence, but not God confidence, which stems from knowing who I am in relationship to him and who God actually is in Jesus. Love was something that would just go away if I was not perfect. I believed that love was kind of a waste of time, to be fully transparent! Everything felt like conditional love, and I couldn't ever seem to be enough for it.

The orphan spirit makes you live like you have to steal your inheritance when you're actually an heir to the kingdom. You try to take it and leave, ending up like the prodigal son but forgetting the One who gave it to you.

Living with an orphan spirit feels like not wanting to depend on anyone. Not trusting groups. Wanting to be a lone wolf all the time and taking pride in your ability to not have to rely on people. I wouldn't ask for help. I'd accept scraps because I felt I didn't need anything, and I trained others to treat me the same way. It led to a lot of control in my life—trying to manage every outcome because I couldn't trust a Father to provide. It's a constant survival mindset.

That's how I perceived it with God. So I thought, "You know what? I fail so many times. And if his love is conditional, I'm just going to stop attempting because it's a waste of my time. I've failed so many times, he's just going to keep pushing me away or pushing back the goalpost."

But I didn't realize I was pushing him away. He was always there; I just didn't want to see him because it didn't match my beliefs about reality and what love is. I had no idea what love really was, until Jesus opened my eyes.

Learning What Love Really Is

Love, real love, is always there, no matter if it's a good time or bad time: "Love is patient, love is kind. It does not envy, it does not boast, it is not proud ... It keeps no record of wrongs" (1 Cor. 13:4–5 NIV).

Above all, God is love (1 John 4:8)! When I read that, it changed so much for me. I kept pushing away the love I was seeking, because I was pushing God away. And he had been showing me patience, kindness, mercy and grace my entire life. He was actually loving me!

If we've experienced people who kept records of wrongs, who were short-tempered, were not patient, or were not kind to us, then we have a distorted view of love. And if we have a distorted view of love, we'll have a distorted view of everything that actually matters in our life, while loving people incorrectly. I've had to spend a *lot* of time undoing these old patterns and ways of relating.

It applies to our creations too. If you're trying to build something you care about, if there's no love in it, you won't be patient and kind with it. You'll be trying to force it. You'll be trying a get-rich-quick scheme. You'll be trying to take a shortcut. You'll compromise yourself for something that isn't truly aligned with you. You'll get mad at yourself for not being at the end result fast enough, which destroys your creative ability. You'll look at your own failures and hold them against yourself because you haven't learned what love actually is. So you keep your own record of wrongs, and that keeps you stuck in a toxic version of yourself.

One of the hardest false agreements for us to break is letting go of "my way." In fact, it's *the* hardest!

I always thought my way was best because I believed I could do anything. My dad did a great job programming that belief: "You can do anything you set your mind to." But it wasn't grounded in a full, tangible God relationship, so it resulted in having pride in my own abilities. I saw myself as a god.

It was in the subtle belief that I was the sole author of my own story, the master of my fate, the captain of my soul. That William Ernest Henley "Invictus" mindset that sounds noble but is actually rebellion dressed in poetry.

Like I said earlier, we do have choice to a degree, but when we align with God, it's not really us. It's the spirit.

Breaking that agreement meant admitting that I wasn't God. That my way wasn't always best. That maybe, just maybe, the Creator of the universe might have better ideas than a dude with an unused business degree and trust issues.

Seeing His Love Move

How you're relating to yourself is how you're relating to the world around you. All your creations, all your interactions, all your relationships. Where you feel scarcity in the world around you and in yourself shows where you feel scarce with God and don't believe that he is abundant, or on your side.

And that is your opportunity to let him in. To no longer be an orphan but to be adopted into the family he has called you to be part of. To recognize your identity as someone who is completely and always loved unconditionally by your Creator, the One who made you, who is only pure Love and can be nothing other.

The biggest shift came as I started to release old, stuck emotions. I was crying at least five times a week to release what was stuck. Years of suppressed grief, anger, and disappointment all came up to be healed. I was weeping on the floor, singing into my karaoke machine, and looking back, even though it sucked, I think it was pretty hilarious.

In those moments of breaking down, I started to see him talk to me through the Bible to comfort me. Whenever I'd listen to worship music, I could actually see and feel the grace he was giving me. I'd feel the love he had for me to allow me to break down without judgment. I was healing by feeling.

It took deep humility and finally admitting that I couldn't do it alone. Like recognizing that my tears weren't weakness but surrender, that my breaking was actually my making.

God is fully good. We get to have his goodness inside us when we're attached to him.

But other than that, we can't have goodness alone because God *is* goodness. If we don't have God in our lives, we don't have goodness. And God is love, which means we are loveless unless we have him with us.

If we don't have love, we don't have life. You're not going to be a person whom you like when you look in the mirror because you haven't learned how to love—if God isn't the biggest part of your life. But what's bigger than focusing on how much we love ourselves is how much we love God, and then you'll feel that love anyway.

Have you ever heard of the word *enlightenment* like the Buddhists use? Well, the true path to "enlightenment" that they're not understanding is . . .

No longer trying to attain it. Only when you stop seeking to actualize yourself and realize that you can only reach your full potential by submission to the Holy Spirit through Jesus Christ do you get there.

But it's not about getting there anyway. It's about getting *him*.

The etymology for *enlightenment* is to be brought "into the light," representing a state of clarity, understanding, and the removal of ignorance.[3] When we put our focus on God, we empower the Holy Spirit inside of us and become that lamp that Jesus talks about. We can't step into the light if we're running away from the source of it, which is Jesus. Otherwise, we remain ignorant.

"Apart from me you can do nothing," Jesus said (John 15:5 NLT). Paul said, "I can do all things through Christ who strengthens me" (Phil. 4:13 NKJV). There's nothing that can be done without God because God is the answer—if you choose to realize that. Only Jesus is "the way, the truth, and the life" (John 14:6 NKJV).

Trust me when I tell you this: I've been *incredibly* ignorant, walking all of the paths except the true way. I thought I found the answer, attained enlightenment, realized Christ consciousness, blah blah blah. All of it ended up being false when I actually experienced the love of Christ, the man-God.

You have to consciously make him part of your life and let him cleanse you, and accept the identity he's placed over you as a son or daughter. In fact, if he chose you, he is a part of your life. But we can put our hands over our eyes or our fingers in our ears and pretend the truth doesn't exist like the Pharisees, making him effectively not a part of it. Even atheists can't escape God!

The Man in the Mirror

Before understanding I was a son of God, I'd look in the mirror and see no identity other than what I was doing on the surface. Empty. Dead. But capable of conquering the world!

My eyes were dark for a long time, like there was nobody home. My skin was dull, lifeless, like I was just existing but not living. I saw a

---

[3] "enlightened," *Vocabulary.com Dictionary,* Vocabulary.com, accessed November 25, 2025, https://www.vocabulary.com/dictionary/enlightened#:~:text=Add%20to%20 list,having%20much%20knowledge%20or%20education.

performer, a faker, someone trying to be everything to everyone but nothing to himself, earning my way to love and validation.

After I understood that I'm a son of God, everything changed. I felt like I had belonging, after taking pride in being a black sheep my entire life. I found lasting purpose, and I knew who I was, and suddenly everything had more meaning. I could see the reasons for the seasons. The struggles had meaning. The journey had a destination that wouldn't fade away.

Now when I look in the mirror, I see someone who is loved not for what he does but for who he is. I see potential not based on my ability but on God's power working through me. I see a son who has an inheritance, not an orphan scrambling for scraps.

And sometimes, it can go back to the old way. But I'm not going to hate myself for it! I just correct my steps and continue on the path forward.

The Choice of Repentance

There's no crazy action step you can take other than coming to repentance, but that's been what our focus has been the entire time you've been reading. You have to acknowledge the areas where you've gone astray, where you've gone lost, where you've missed the mark—which is what sin is. Own up to that. Be honest about that.

Talk to God. He's not going to punish you for being truthful with him. He took away that price through Jesus. He wants to redeem you, restore you, and heal your relationship with him. But you have to make the choice to want to come to him and choose to let yourself be rewired. You have to be open about it. And through that, he can heal you.

When you finally repent—which means not just to change your thinking but to change your actions, too, to change your way of being and the way you do things—when you do that and start to turn toward who you're meant to become, that's when the identity becomes clearer, and you walk with purpose.

Repentance is the most noble thing we can do—for ourselves, for those around us, and for God.

Even when you felt you didn't deserve it, he was still with you. Even in your lows, he was with you. In the highs, he was with you. Even the times you forgot him when you were winning, he was still cheering you on. Even when you were down and didn't want help, or didn't know whom to talk to, he was trying to get your attention to help you out.

He's always been there.

When you can feel that abundance of love—the ultimate fuel, the only thing that can truly last for eternity—that's when you can experience life the way it was meant to be lived. From the lens you were designed to view it from.

Whenever you feel disconnected, it's an opportunity to look at where you're putting something as a higher priority than the One who gave that thing to you. That thing is taking your attention and peace away from you by masquerading as God, making you feel empty and lost, when all you have to do is turn your head and your heart toward the Father.

Seeing the Unseen Love

"Seeing the unseen," what God said to me, isn't just trying to see invisible things. No, it's about seeing the love that is moving through your life when you previously couldn't. It's seeing the abundance of it when you've been so used to seeing through a lens of scarcity.

It's changing your outlook on situations to see them with a new perspective, and tapping into the subtle realm that is behind everything our physical eyes can see. It's being able to discern cause and effect, being able to rewrite a future pattern because you understand a previous one. It's knowing how to see God moving when those around you don't.

When you can see that love, you can start to perceive situations, events, and people in a way they haven't been seen before, because you're no longer enamored with, or attached to, surface-level appearances. That's what it means to have God's eyes on a situation—because God is love, and whatever God views, he views through true love.

Start to agree with God's promises and God's truth more than your own circumstances, and you'll start to win the battle that's been trying to claim your soul. You are not what happened to you. You are not your failures. You are not your successes. You are not what people said about you. You are not even what you've said about yourself.

You are who God says you are. A son. A daughter. Loved, chosen, and redeemed.

You're worthy. Not because of anything you've done, but because of who he is and what he's done.

When you can see yourself through his eyes—really see it, not just know it intellectually but feel it in your bones—everything changes. The mirror stops being a judge and becomes a reminder of grace. Your mistakes stop being verdicts and become testimonies. Your pain stops being pointless and becomes purposeful. It's seeing "I wonder what God will do next" at every place you had put a period. You start moving with childlike wonder and curiosity.

Now that you have a clear glimpse of who you are and who God is, it's time to embody that identity and start walking with purpose and divine sight so you can bring this truth to fruition.

Because seeing isn't enough. Now you must become.

Chapter 5 Implementation: Week 6

Teaching Point

Now seeing God clearly, you discover the secret: Everything in your life has been reflecting your internal relationship with him. Your frustrating patterns, your repeated struggles—they're all mirrors showing you where you still see yourself as an orphan instead of an heir.

Mindset Shift

From "I am someone who struggles" to "I am God's beloved child." The second one will carry you, no matter the circumstance.

Prayer

"Father, I'm tired of seeing myself through broken mirrors. Show me who I really am through your eyes. Break every false agreement I've made—from childhood wounds, from failures, from lies I believed about myself. I renounce my orphan spirit and receive my identity as your child. Help me see the love that's been moving through my life all along. I choose your truth over my history. Transform how I see myself so I can reflect you clearly. I am your [son/daughter], and that changes everything. In Jesus's name, amen."

Scriptures to Meditate On

- "See what kind of love the Father has given to us, that we should be called children of God; and so we are" (1 John 3:1 ESV).

- "Therefore, if anyone is in Christ, he is a new creation; old things have passed away; behold, all things have become new" (2 Cor. 5:17 NKJV).

- "I will be a Father to you, and you will be my sons and daughters, says the Lord Almighty" (2 Cor. 6:18 NKJV).

Action Steps

1. **False agreement inventory.** Write down beliefs about yourself that contradict God's Word. On another sheet, write what God says instead. Example: "I'm unworthy" → "I am chosen and dearly loved" (Col. 3:12, paraphrased). Burn the paper with the lies and keep the one with God's truth, praying words of power over it.

2. **Mirror exercise.** Stand in front of a mirror for five minutes. First two minutes: Notice every critical thought. Next three minutes: Speak God's truth over yourself out loud. "I am a [son/daughter] of the Most High God. I am loved. I am chosen. I am enough because he is enough." Let yourself feel the part of yourself that holds back, be with it, and continue on until you are no longer resisting.

3. **The relationship reflection.** List three recurring relationship problems. For each one, ask: "How is this reflecting something in me?" Then ask God to heal that area. Watch how your external relationships shift as your internal relationship with him deepens.

CHAPTER 6 DISCERNMENT IS SIGHT IN MOTION

Now that we've unlocked that clarity in ourselves, learning how to do it daily, we're going to learn how to increase our discernment, awareness, and the grounded energy we're embodying.

How do we increase our discernment and channel our energy into spiritual growth? Here's the first thing I want to ask you: Where are you putting your attention? Because wherever you put your intention will receive your attention. And whatever you put your attention on becomes your god. What holds your attention controls your direction.

So it all comes down to the questions: What are you worshiping? What are you putting your energy into and making your god? That distraction will be one of the biggest roadblocks to you seeing clearly.

The Gods I Didn't Know I Served

This is something you have to really ask yourself: "What are my motives?"

By "motives," I mean why you do certain things. For a lot of my life, I didn't realize how much I was making fear and doubt my god. I was making betrayal and abandonment my god. I was making money and my success and self-reliance my god. Romantic relationships—I was making all of them my gods.

I wasn't putting my full attention on the God who was really with me. I was just putting my attention on the things he gave to me. The things that were good in my eyes. Or the things I thought I needed instead of what he knew I needed.

I realized they were more god than God when I saw that they were determining my actions more than he was. One of the biggest moments was when my business felt like it was falling apart and I was doing everything I could to fix it. Freaking out. Panicking. Working sixteen-hour days, trying to control every outcome.

My wake-up call was when I exhausted myself trying to control outcomes. I was on the floor of my home, completely depleted, heart pumping from too much caffeine, mind racing with strategies that weren't working. And in that moment of complete burnout, I heard a simple question in my spirit: "Why do I feel like I need to force things?"

The answer was obvious. I was trusting my ability to fix things more than God's ability to guide things.

What Discernment Really Is

Discernment really comes down to spiritual critical thinking. It's the ability to see a situation for what it is, to pierce the truth inside of it and cut through the noise so you can see what God is doing, where he's taking you, and where the root of things stem from. It helps you from getting caught in the distractions of the outside world.

The only way to really gain it is that, first, you must have the desire to want it. You have to have a heart for God and the desire to want to ask him to give you discernment. That's why David could mess up and do all the things he did—because at the end of the day, his heart was still seeking God. God said he's "a man after my own heart" (Acts 13:22 NLT). When our heart is seeking God, we're going to try and find the truth, and God is the truth. That's why David was quick to repent.

If there's still stuff inside you that you haven't let go of or haven't repented for, ask yourself: "How much does my heart actually want to know the truth? How much do I really, really want to know God? How much do I actually want to see?"

Because the more you have the intention of putting your energy into the truth, the clearer God is going to become. The more you're going to gain his eyes naturally because you're using this spiritual critical-thinking skill to look into a situation and say, "What does God see here? God, what are you seeing in this moment?"

That requires humility and a desire to wait for him instead of bum-rushing it. It's still possible to see yet not want to submit to what he shows you.

Have you seen *The Matrix*? You know the guy eating the steak? He saw things clearly, but he liked the steak more!

The Stillness We Avoid

To get clear, you need to sit down and take the time to be still. Plain and simple.

The stillness is where God speaks to us most clearly, but we want to avoid it as much as possible. Because in that stillness, all the emotions we have not wanted to confront come to the surface. That's the Holy Spirit guiding us inside. It's also where we have to face the truth itself.

In that stillness, get a journal and ask yourself where your attention goes most often. What are you thinking about the most? What are you focusing on the most?

Are you focusing on negative outcomes? Then you're probably worshiping anxiety, fear, doubt. Are you thinking about the qualities of God? Are you asking yourself where he's taking you? Are you in awe of him? Then your heart is aimed at the one place that's going to get you where you want to go.

Journaling is great because it will help you get all of your thoughts out of your head and organized in front of your eyes, which naturally helps organize your brain. Take it out, organize, feed it back in. It makes things super clear.

My brain is very ADHD (self-diagnosed)—it's an engine that's constantly running and always has stuff coming out of it. When it's on, it's on 200 percent. So journaling helps me to organize my thoughts and get them out in front of me so I can see what my thoughts even are in the first place.

Because when there's so much inside our head and we don't know what to even look at, that jumbled mess can get confusing. By journaling, we write down in front of us and have a physical visualization of what's going on in our minds, which allows us to have the awareness of choice. We can see what we're obsessed with, and what's blocking our view.

The Patterns That Bind Us

Next up, look at your patterns.

Your patterns that you may have learned for survival or what you've thought love is—those patterns can feel comfortable to us. We keep seeking out situations and circumstances and creating them where those patterns get to come to fruition as a physical experience in front of our eyes. Whether it's a relationship, a creation, you name it.

Because those are so comfortable and because we have an emotional attachment to those experiences, they can suck us in. That's when we start to lose sight of God. We lose sight of the truth. Familiarity has an appealing draw that disconnects us from the uncertainty required of faith.

Ask yourself: "Is my heart wanting the truth that may be uncomfortable? Or does my heart want an emotional delusion that feels comfortable and I've known my entire life?" Because one of those is going to keep you stuck where you've been, and one is going to get you to where you're trying to go.

While you ask yourself those things, look at your actions. Look at the actions of people around you. Where are you going most frequently? Where is your money going? Have you looked at what you're buying on your credit card? Whom are you hanging out with?

Are any of those things fruitful in a positive way? If you're consistently seeing negative fruit, that's a problem. You're in some pattern that's not aligned with the truth. If you're truly seeking God first, and still seeing areas of your life that aren't even a tiny bit fruitful, then you may not actually be seeking God first. It's not even about the fruits; they're simply indicators of your inputs. The fruit is the output.

Do you want to truly discern the actions and words of those around you? Ask God first, but then also make sure you're actually discerning the truth in yourself first so that you're clear. How do you know if what is in front of you is good or bad if you're blind?

It's less important to worry about what other people are doing if you're not first looking at yourself. That willingness to die to yourself is service on its own.

Matthew 7:3–5 NIV states:

Why do you look at the speck of sawdust in your brother's eye and pay no attention to the plank in your own eye? How can you say to your brother, "Let me take the speck out of your eye," when all the time there is a plank in your own eye? You hypocrite, first take the plank out of your own eye, and then you will see clearly to remove the speck from your brother's eye.

Jesus said it first!

Building from Wounds

As I was growing my own business—my supplement brand, the Stampede Network—I realized how much I'd been doing it from a wounded place. It was out of performance when I started. I didn't have as full a relationship with God as I do now, so all these things I was building were actually running on the wrong fuel source. Every time I'd have success, I felt good. Every time I plateaued or went down a little bit, I'd freak out.

I had no emotional stability. Why? Because God was not at the base of it. Fear and doubt were. It's like trying to launch a rocket into space on gasoline. That ain't gonna go too far, partner!

It felt like everything I did had those elements attached to it. I had a constant thought that everything would fall apart, no matter what was going on. My operational management was aggressive and moved in waves. Emotional pendulums were part of daily life because my stability was linked to the results I had. If they were down, I was ultra down. It was like a ping pong ball bouncing between ceiling and floor.

One day meant record sales, and I was on top of the world. The next day meant a dip, and I was convinced we were going bankrupt. My team never knew which version of me they'd get—the visionary leader or the panicked micromanager.

I had to really look at myself deeply and look at the patterns going on. The more they emotionally trapped me, the more I was making them my god.

You have to look at what has an emotional hold over you. If it has a hold over you, that's an area where you're not free. And without that internal feeling of freedom, you will not be able to have true discernment. You have not allowed Jesus into that area to be your source of peace. Without peace in that area, it's hard to discern correctly outside yourself in similar situations.

The Truth Behind the Curtain

Discernment is amplified when you can be unattached to the emotional experience of what you're going through. You may feel it. You may experience it. But you are not the emotion. The discernment is allowing you to see what's being said under the surface. Where is wisdom guiding you in this moment? What's the truth behind the curtain? What's at the root of this feeling, which in the end is just a symptom?

There may be a show happening on the main stage in front of that curtain, but behind the scenes, there's a director, and there's a script that's playing out. And if you want to change the show, you've got to go behind the curtain to talk to who is running it and writing it.

I had to step back and sit in the tension of not knowing how things would turn out—which, by the way, never ends when we have someone named God. I had to surrender control of part of my business to my partner, Brian, so that he could help me lead, which I was delaying because I didn't trust anyone. That meant giving up equity, which in my head meant my family would never have money. That meant letting go of being the sole decision-maker. That meant trusting someone else with my baby . . . my complex, digital baby.

Get clarity on those thoughts in yourself, the things you find your emotional stability in that aren't God, and start deeply asking yourself: "Why do I keep getting sucked into this idea? Why do I keep getting sucked into this thought? Why does this bring me comfort?"

The thing we spend the most time thinking about is the thing we love the most. Our mind feeds the heart, and the heart determines where we find ourselves.

What it's going to require from you is extremely radical self-accountability, which not many people want to use. Not many people want to be fully accountable for their emotions. They want to blame. They want to put them on other people. They want to rely on others or things to let them feel good emotionally. We all have this tendency, but how fast do you repent from it?

This is how an addiction happens. We have to remove those addictions in our lives because what they're doing is becoming an altar and a false god for a feeling we don't want to feel. They give us a temporary sense of feeling relief, a quick hit of tranquility rather than a lasting one. If you remove that addiction, there's a void where the feeling you're trying to cover up comes to the surface. And that's what needs to be felt and met. Don't be scared of it; embrace it with intimate love. Intimacy can be restated as "into me I see," so allow yourself to be seen by seeing yourself fully and being there for those wounded parts of yourself seeking redemption. This requires presence.

Action Without Direction

One of the other things people get confused with discernment is they think it comes just from action alone. You hear all the time in the entrepreneur world, "Take action, and clarity comes later." Yes, it does. But you still need faith and you need a connection to God. Otherwise, your movement is out of target, and you're playing pinball.

Just because you're moving doesn't mean you're actually being led by the truth or moving anywhere meaningful. Sight must precede accurate motion. Imagine bowling with no bumpers and your eyes closed. God can get you that strike, of course, but what's the point of even doing that when you have eyes? We can move, but how much energy are we wasting if we're not moving in the direction we want to go?

Another way to put it is that it's like being a ship at sea. You could be a few degrees off crossing the Atlantic, and you could end up in a completely different country than the one you're trying to get to because you don't have the right targeting.

If your heart is not on God first, you're listening to the wrong instructions. They could be from the trauma in your mind, old limiting beliefs, addictions, or Satan whispering in your ear—this is why it's so important to listen to God and read the Bible. In the Bible, you're going to start to gain awareness of how God speaks and what his thoughts sound like. You'll gain insight on the targeting of where he wants you to go and who he wants you to be. If you don't have an ideal to embody and shoot for, you're lost at sea. After you absorb and meditate on his words, when he brings a thought to mind, you'll be able to know if it's aligned with love and God.

If he didn't say it, it ain't it!

When Success Becomes Your Master

One of the biggest roadblocks we deal with is that we strive, meaning we carve our own path while usually ignoring the peace and timing of God. It's sneaky, because when you're making progress, it feels good . . . until our pride disconnects us from him without us realizing it. We strive for things and outcomes and achievements to feel like we matter or like we mean something. But in reality, when we realize our identity is a son or daughter of God, we don't have to strive. We're already loved. We already have everything we need in God. Do you want the applause of man? Or the Creator of man?

Instead of striving, we need to chill out and be directed by God. If you're to strive for anything, strive to be as present as possible with

God for as many moments of the day as you can. You naturally will take the right steps.

Use the Bible as a tool for a mastery of discipleship—because that's what it is. It means Basic Instructions Before Leaving Earth. It's not just a book. It's a lens into how God sees things, and a guide to prepare for where we're meant to go in the next life. Prayer is not just talk. It's alignment with how God sees things. It's aligning your heart with his way.

The Gift of Awareness

As you seek more of God in his Word, in his presence, he starts to increase your awareness, and your awareness of the spirit world grows. Awareness is a gift from God, a by-product of having your spiritual eyes opened. As you seek him ("God, help me see with your eyes into this situation") and gain awareness of what's truly happening under the surface, that's him helping you out. Because "the hearing ear and the seeing eye, the Lord has made them both" (Prov. 20:12 NKJV).

There have been times where I've sat in silent meditation and prayer for an hour every single morning for months straight, letting the emotions and feelings move through my body, noticing with awareness the subtle energy inside and outside of me. I was learning how to feel the substance of Spirit, just like I can touch a wall with my hand. I would consciously notice inner resistance or an energy block and let it move through my body. I'd ask myself: "What am I feeling right now? What is this feeling telling me?"

Then the Holy Spirit inside me—which is inside all of us who are saved—would guide me into feeling that emotion I didn't want to feel. It was an intercession on my behalf, experienced through groanings. This was part of the process of washing the inside of the cup so that the outside could be clean (Matt. 23:26). On the other side of it, I would have insight into an emotional block I was going through. A feeling or a way of relating that was not healthy or good. An area where I didn't feel free. A place where I was hiding myself or not expressing myself, and not surrendering to God.

Many times, this was followed by tears, anger, or another emotional purge. Each time, it was good, and I was cleaner than when I entered. I would observe myself having an emotional release, and even though it sucked at times, I would be able to see from a higher point of awareness that "this is good."

We can always find gratitude for what God is doing among the turmoil of life, and it's easier when he becomes the prize we're looking for.

The Grieving We Avoid

Some things so many of us are scared to feel when we read the Bible are the negative emotions that come up when we do read it—the convictions. Because through those convictions, it tells us where what we have been doing is not fully in alignment with love and God. These moments are doorways into grief, if we allow them to be—which, by the way, is a good thing if it's not grieving the spirit!

Why? Because in grief, you are shedding an old identity and story; you are able to release what has been for what is to come. This is healing.

Going through the grieving process, though—it freaking sucks. I've laid on the floor, rolling around like a baby, crying and screaming to the sky for God to help me move through the pain. Snot and tears have poured down my face like Niagara Falls. But I also knew at the same time that it was for my greater good. I had the awareness to feel the painful emotion but also know that it was a good thing.

There were feelings of guilt and shame from doing things I knew weren't aligned with my character but couldn't stop doing. I didn't have the strength on my own to let go of them.

Most of the time, we need God to give us that extra nudge if we're not jacked up fully on faith. We need the feeling of knowing "I shouldn't do this" when we still do it—whether from pride, fear, ego, or a need for survival.

Paul says in Romans 7:15–20 NIV:

> I do not understand what I do. For what I want to do I do not do, but what I hate I do. And if I do what I do not want to do, I agree that the law is good. As it is, it is no longer I myself who does it, but it is sin living in me. For I know that good itself does not dwell in me, that is, in my sinful nature. For I have the desire to do what is good, but I cannot carry it out. For I do not do the good I want to do, but the evil I do not want to do—this I keep on doing. Now if I do what I do not want to do, it is no longer I who do it, but it is sin living in me that does it.

Yeah, dude. I felt that—exactly how confusing it is! Through the grieving process, the toxic beliefs and patterns clear out.

A good example of this was the Jesus deliverance incident I talked about earlier in the book, when I felt old stagnant energy come out of me. On the other side, I was able to feel the emotions and deeper wounds clear out from my body, fully surrendering to Jesus.

When the dense negativity cleared out—that emotion that was creating a whirlpool inside me—it allowed the waters to be still, just like Jesus with the disciples when they were in the middle of the storm on the boat. The waters were crazy before this happened. There was a giant storm. And as soon as Jesus rebuked them—as soon as the truth came into the picture—there was stillness. He calmed the wind, all of the false beliefs, which allowed the emotions in the water to calm down.

This is what happens when we let him into our life. When we let the truth into our life, the emotional storm inside us calms down, and we can finally see where we're at and what's in front of us. He gives us supernatural peace.

But here's the thing: You need to do your job to invite him in!

The Seven-Day Vision

Something else you can do to help open your eyes is to choose one verse about wisdom, vision, or something that stands out to you regarding discernment. Whatever comes up, wherever God leads you after you pray for him to reveal it, meditate on it for seven days. Just recite it in your head over and over. Ask him to expand your sight and show you what he wants you to see while giving you awareness of what it's really saying. You want to chew on it like a cow chews on cud. Dissect it and contemplate it. Ask yourself, "What is really at the root of this? What do each of the words truly mean in this verse? What are their etymologies? Where does this apply?"

As you chew on it, you eventually swallow it, right? Just like food, it becomes a part of your being. You then are able to start embodying what you previously only had in your head.

Know that as you increase your discernment, there's one thing that's going to be the biggest change in your life: The more you see the root of what's in front of you, the more precisely you're going to move.

Every act of intentional worship, contemplation, and seeking of his heart sharpens your spiritual motion. When you see God clearly, you can see the truth clearly. Seeing him equals seeing what he is made of—the truth—in all facets of life. And when you're seeking him with all of your heart, that means the actions and steps you take are going to be guided by the One who created every possible direction. This knowing leads to confidence and becomes an anchor; there is not necessarily a wrong path when you're in a right way of being. You have more certainty, clarity, and intentionality, because you know you're walking in purpose.

And purpose isn't a place to get to. It's something that you embody.

Divine Confirmation

Before writing this book, I had no idea what "See the unseen" meant for years. Then I gained deeper insight, and out of nowhere, I just felt called to write a book. I didn't really know about what, but this was just what came up. It was natural, and I felt peace with it. I mean, I've been living it out for over half a decade!

Even though I didn't always understand what was going on, I just kept seeking God. I kept seeking his wisdom. I kept seeking the truth. I kept moving with faith while staying connected to him, because I knew he would reveal it to me over time.

I went to my current church for the first time before writing this book, on Father's Day. The pastor talked about a man seeing himself how God sees him, as a son.

But it went deeper. The pastor was talking about our roles as men of God to be spiritual fathers and what spiritual fatherhood is. He said that as fathers, we need to "see the unseen" in our homes.

I felt immediately that God was calling me home into a relationship with him as my Father. He said that to me in the meditation I mentioned before, years ago, and I realized my identity as a son rather than an orphan spirit. Just like everything he does, it came at the perfect time. He told me who he was to me at that moment, my Father. I felt like I had purpose and knew what I was here to do—a big part being reconciling the hearts of men to God and restoring that deep love through a healed relationship.

I knew in that moment God was with me while I was writing this book. I know he's been helping me write this book you're reading because of the alignment, the synchronicities, the flow that's come from it. I would be watching a podcast, then the exact page I wrote that day would be talked about. I wouldn't even be looking for it! The purpose, the awareness—everything feels intentional and powerful because I'm seeking him to write this book. I didn't realize how fatherless I felt, but hearing those words that day gave me confirmation of who he is to me.

Even through the hard times when I've messed up, he's still been my Father: "'Is not Israel still my son, my darling child?' says the LORD.

'I often have to punish him, but I still love him. That's why I long for him and surely will have mercy on him'" (Jer. 31:20 NLT).

He always loves his children through both the ups and downs of life. And you are one of God's children, so know that he loves you too.

Spiritual Warfare Is Real

The hardest thing you're going to do when walking out your purpose isn't actually walking out your purpose. From my experience, it's staying spiritually connected and knowing how to fight spiritual warfare without losing connection to your God-given identity.

The closer we get to God, the more the enemy hates us. There's a target painted on your because you're becoming spiritually hot. There are going to be distractions that come. They're going to pull your mind away. They're going to try to fill you with doubt and fear, saying, "You can't do it. You're not meant to do this."

Do you trust what's happening in the play, or the Director of it?

Turn your will to God in prayer. Say, "God, realign my eyes. Realign my heart. Help me know you. Help me seek you and recognize the authority you have given me. Remove the blocks in myself that prevent me from seeing the truth in this moment. Expose where I'm not free, and come into that area to transform it. Help remove inside of me any pattern that is not meant to be there."

Keep a log of how he responds. Journal. Start taking note of your journey. Write down spiritual markers, like memorials, in a separate journal so that you don't forget. This is one of the best tactics to separate us from God: to convince us that he wasn't ever there for us in the first place.

Rebuke each thought that tempts you to doubt God and his goodness. Brutally go after it by using the Word to back your prayers and knowing that if anything is in alignment with God's will, then it will be answered.

Each time God comes into your life more viscerally, start documenting how he's moving. The more you've seen him move in your past, the more it's going to give you faith to move forward in the future. You'll know he's shown up for you, but if you forget, you'll have proof. He's shown up for you in so many different ways, but the distraction and rush of life can get our hearts caught up on the wrong things, and we forget he ever existed.

He lends you his eyes as you seek his heart.

It's not about receiving the gift of discernment; it's about seeking the One who can see all things. Through that, you'll gain sight anyway.

Fear Disguised as Discernment

Another huge factor that blocks us from actually discerning is worshiping fear more than faith. For me, this has been an addiction that I've had in my life. I had certain beliefs about situations, people, events, things that I carried into certain situations, even believing that I'm not "doing enough" to get to heaven, falling into religiosity instead of leaning on Jesus. Because of that, I would let fear rule me. Every time I would feel fear in my body, mind, heart—I would not go through it. I would avoid it. Then I would shut it down by feeling "enough" from my striving. There was no rest, just momentum. It's still something that can surface in times of stress!

I'd feel like I was in a safe little bubble. But what I was doing in reality was just avoiding moving through fear and moving in a way where God could work a miracle in my life.

Every time we avoid moving through our fear, we're insulting God. We're telling him that he is not bigger than our fears. Moving through fear is ironically letting go of "trying" to move through it and instead putting all of your faith in God. It's an innate part of being human to feel fear, so don't be ashamed of this. Instead, take it to him.

One of the things that can happen is that Satan, the deceiver and the liar, can convince us that our fear is discernment. He'll say, "Oh no, don't go there. Don't talk to this person. Don't do this because you're going to get hurt."

Are you sure about that? Is there any actual threat? Are you feeling fear as you do it? Are you feeling actual conviction that's rooted in peace? Because if you're feeling fear in your body as you hear that, guess what? That's not God.

Yes, the Holy Spirit can warn us, but if we're feeling paralyzing fear, it's not God.

We can think we have discernment when in reality, we're just avoiding wanting to confront feelings inside ourselves that are all rooted back into fear. Then we view from that lens, and we think what we're discerning is "true," but it's only true to that paradigm we're viewing it from. We can create a legalistic standard that's rooted in past pain or a human interpretation of holiness, but it lacks God's grace. That's the lens we take when we believe that everything comes from our effort alone and we don't trust God's truth, the only truth, over what we think is true.

When we're living in fear, we're not actually living in love or faith, as fear disconnects us from what connects us to God. Without love being injected into each moment, your discernment isn't true. It's simply a projected mask.

The Mirror of Truth

My romantic relationships I've experienced have taught me a valuable lesson. When someone calls something out in me, it's not necessarily a way to control me. Yes, sometimes it can be a projection, but for the most part, they have been a mirror for pointing out where I have been trying to control things, ironically, and where I've not been in alignment with the truth myself. Because I wasn't always in alignment, I projected onto a lot of people my own darkness and thought that what I saw in myself was truer than what she saw. But

I was viewing myself from a wounded lens, and therefore the world around me too. I was blinded to my own areas of darkness and was addicted to them.

Everything we do, everything we see, stems from who we are.

I was avoiding my own accountability that I expected from the person in front of me. I had to be humbled by periods of loss and deep pain for me to clear out the blocks that were created by wounds so I could finally see clearly. Again, I needed to feel it to heal it.

All our blocks come from emotional incoherence and false beliefs that have become strongholds, and they are like putting mud over a telescope. We think it's dark, and we can't see very far, so we think that's how reality is. We need to remove the blocks and our sight naturally improves.

You have to be very honest with yourself and look at what you're scared of: Where am I living in fear? What is this decision in front of me? Am I doing it because I'm scared of failure or some negative outcome? Or am I doing it because I'm moving with faith? Am I making a decision because I just don't want to take responsibility for myself and face my own emotions? Or have I truly looked so deeply at myself and come to terms with my own wounds and things holding me back, that I still feel I need to do it?

Self-inquiry, checked by the Bible and the Holy Spirit, is the way back into alignment.

One path is driven by fear, and one is driven by faith. It's only through that deep self-analysis, with God's help to gain awareness, that you can create the space for true discernment.

The Judge Must First Judge Himself

Discernment is given to the judge. The judge can discern what is true. He knows the right from the wrong, the true from the false.

And if you're not able to judge yourself correctly, how are you going to judge anything around you correctly? You can't.

A big factor is a deep, cancerous type of wound in the spirit called unforgiveness. Unforgiveness leads to bitterness. Until we remove unforgiveness, we can't see clearly. And God doesn't forgive us, either, until we do, so we walk around blind and angry. We don't have our prayers answered. We remain stuck.

This all comes back to humility.

We have to choose to forgive. If we avoid things, we can't forgive. We can be offended in a moment by something. We can have an emotion that makes us uncomfortable and think, "I don't want to think about this right now. I don't want to look at it." So we shut it down. We repress it.

Because we repress it, it gets irritated in our body. It builds up internally and festers. Then we get mad. We get angry because the pain continues to spread throughout us. Then we get bitter because we never actually had the courage to say what we're feeling. A sense of injustice solidifies, and we get mad at everything. Then we want to take it out on those around us without ever realizing subconsciously that we're just mad at ourselves.

Because we do this, our heart becomes numb. We lose compassion and love because we're choosing to act out of love. We become the embodiment of a cancer cell . . . and you don't think that may play a part in the disease itself? This isn't all people, of course, but it's something to think about.

After all of this is when we just start to feel pain internally. We're suffering. We feel spiritually, emotionally, and physically wrecked. God allows us to go through this as a consequence of us not letting things go with other people and persistently being unforgiving.

Until you let go of those things you're holding onto that are painful, you can't bring in the things that bring you joy. Discern the truth first by seeing if this is true for you. Ask God where you're not for-giving those around you.

Say, "Father, I know in my heart I have hidden sins. Please show me where I have hidden unforgiveness and bitterness. Show me what I'm avoiding facing internally. Show me what situation this pain has come from, in Jesus's name."

You must dig into the darkness and dissolve it with light. That's when you start to truly see things clearly.

Seeing What God Is Really Doing

Whenever you look back into the past, you need to take inventory and ask yourself what was being formed in you. The more you remember how God transformed you and used your circumstances for your development, the more you'll be able to see it moving forward.

Eternity is timeless, so to see with the eyes of eternity means that eyes aware of what happened in the past are similar to eyes that see the future. It's not about seeing forward or backward; it's about taking your perspective from the ground up into the sky so that you can see everything below from a higher vantage point.

God is not bound by time, and our brains contain a mind that is able to interact with a higher dimension than the one we're standing in. Think about it: How are you able to put your awareness on your past as you read these words, and also imagine into the future? You're able to transcend time in your mind, to a degree.

That means that we can imagine, thanks to God's gift of the mind, everything in the past, present, and future as if it's one continuous stream. We can take an entire timeline and place it in front of our eyes with our imagination, if we want to. When you start to take this perspective in any hard situation, you create not only emotional detachment, but also the space to see the bigger picture.

Things seemed to be breaking apart, but through God's promises, they were falling into place. By dropping into humility, you can see in your life how he was loosening your dependence on those things around you for security so you could lean on him instead.

If God is super zoomed out, he's also super zoomed in. Part of the benefits of him being omnipresent and omniscient!

We can follow in his footsteps. What does this mean in action?

In daily conversations, it's listening to the words I say and what others say, while listening for what the emotional context is behind the words. I zoom out to look at the situation, how the person in front of me and I are both a part of it, and see what the higher truth is. I listen to what is really being communicated from the heart of who is speaking to me at the time, without being attached to it.

Through hearing the emotional context, you can hear the truth of what's actually being said. This happens more over time as you allow yourself to be empathetic to your own emotional experience. You cut through the noise, to zoom in while zooming out.

To see the truth and know the truth is to be able to tell what is or is not a lie. This takes a higher perspective, but a closer one as well. Because discernment is more than knowing. It's moving rightly and seeing clearly. It's not just awareness; it's God-fueled direction.

And when you fix your eyes on him through attention, scripture, prayer, and worship, seeking the truth from all perspectives and comparing them to his—your sight becomes sharp, and your steps become Spirit-led.

The journey from spiritual blindness to discernment isn't about gaining a new ability. It's about aligning with the One who sees all.

As you seek his heart, he lends you his eyes.

As you surrender your false gods, he becomes your true North.

As you release your emotional and mental blocks, his truth flows clearly through you.

Now you're ready to understand the final piece—how to live with this sight daily, not as a burden but as a gift.

Chapter 6 Implementation (Week 7)

Teaching Point

With clear vision of God and self in relation, discernment naturally activates—it's not about acquiring a skill but removing the mud from your telescope. Those emotions you've been avoiding aren't obstacles; they're the very pathway to the clarity you've been desperately seeking.

Mindset Shift

From "I need to develop discernment" to "Discernment flows when I'm emotionally clear and in alignment with God."

Prayer

"God, I confess I've made fear, success, relationships, and control my gods. I've worshiped the gifts instead of the Giver. Help me see what has an emotional hold on me so I can surrender it to you. Give me spiritual critical thinking to cut through the noise and see what you're really doing. I'm tired of fear disguised as discernment. I want your truth, not mine, even when it requires grieving what I've held onto. Align my sight with yours. Help me move not just with action but also with accuracy. Show me where I need to forgive. Clear the mud from my glasses so I can see clearly. In Jesus's name, amen."

Scriptures to Meditate On

- "The hearing ear and the seeing eye, the Lord has made them both" (Prov. 20:12 NKJV).

- "But solid food is for the mature, who by constant use have trained themselves to distinguish good from evil" (Heb. 5:14 NIV).

- "Trust in the Lord with all your heart and lean not on your own understanding; in all your ways submit to him, and he will make your paths straight" (Prov. 3:5–6 NIV).

Action Steps

1. **False god inventory.** List what gets most of your mental energy daily (money, relationships, success, fear). Next to each, write how it shows up in your actions. Circle your biggest false god. Fast from it for seven days—redirect that attention to God every time it pulls at you.

2. **Emotional block release.** Set aside an hour. Sit in silence and ask: "What am I feeling that I don't want to feel?" Let whatever comes up fully surface. Don't judge it. Feel it completely. Journal what comes through on the other side. This is removing mud from your telescope.

3. **Seven-day scripture meditation.** Choose one verse about wisdom or discernment. Write it on note cards and place them everywhere. Meditate on it for seven days, asking God to reveal deeper meaning. Document what he shows you each day. Watch how your spiritual sight sharpens.

CHAPTER 7 THE POWER AND PITFALL OF SENSITIVITY

You know one of the biggest lies we've been told in our world growing up? That sensitivity is a weakness. Especially for men. Women aren't really told this as much, but they can be, depending on whether their fathers were connected to their emotions or not. But men, especially in our culture, are generally told that sensitivity is a weak thing.

Many guys go their entire life shutting down their emotions and thinking they can't be real about them. And this is part of the biggest disconnect we experience with God. We think that since we have to hide our emotions with our parents, especially our dads, that means we have to do the same thing with God.

So we put this shell on and start performing. Trying to force ourselves to live a hollow existence because we're shutting down our emotional experience and only keeping the parts that look good on the surface. But those repressed feelings start to build up in the body. The disease of dis-ease of those emotions causes you to get sick. Then that comes out as anger, bitterness, resentment, and frustration, and you force yourself through life.

Unlike what society tells you, sensitivity is actually a strength. Obviously, it doesn't mean to be a limp noodle, but we do need to allow ourselves to feel the full range of emotions.

If we don't have the capacity to feel the depths of "negative" emotions, how would we be able to feel the depth of positive ones? They're all just on a feeling spectrum. It's not black or white. Emotions become idols when we worship them, but we free ourselves from our rule when we simply . . . allow them.

It's so simple, but the most complex thing we humans will ever do. If you aren't even sensitive to yourself, how can you be sensitive to anyone else? It's like a magnet that tries to shut itself down from being a magnet. You naturally magnetize things. Shutting that down is against your innate nature.

Sensitivity is the ability to tap into the unseen realms and feel what is going on spiritually. Without awareness of subtle energy, you're just flesh.

The School of Emotional Shutdown

As I was growing up, my parents had a lot of conflict in stressful times, just as other parents can and do. But seeing that, I never learned a healthy model of conflict resolution or how to process emotions. I was taught, through watching, that it was safer to keep the feelings I felt locked down because I couldn't trust the emotional reaction of the person in front of me. They resolved theirs privately, which is cool, but it left me wondering what was happening behind closed doors.

Every raised voice became a warning. Every slammed door became a lesson. Every tense silence taught me that emotions were dangerous things that made people unpredictable. So I learned to read the room like my survival depended on it—because emotionally, when I was a kid, it did.

This turned into a lot of suppressed anger and resentment. It made me demonize my own emotional experience until I finally gained consciousness of this in my twenties. I believed that God didn't want to see those "dark" parts of me and that I would be punished for showing them.

Enter the performance mindset.

This led to me having nice-guy syndrome while also secretly wanting to get something back from or control the person in front of me unconsciously. I was manipulative without even consciously trying to be. I'd be agreeable on the surface while calculating underneath. I'd say yes when I meant no. I'd smile when I was seething, all because I thought being "good" meant never having difficult emotions.

As you read this, keep in mind that I take full emotional responsibility. We can't blame others for ourselves, even if they can contribute to it. There has to be a mindset shift where we start to take the perspective of "If I'm feeling something bad, it's to teach me something good." It's a martial art of its own.

The Trauma Response We Call a Gift

Here's the one thing I want to warn you about. A lot of people confuse being sensitive with being emotionally fragile. That's not true. We still have to be strong and have a spirit of self-control inside us.

You didn't see Jesus falling apart all the time. Yes, he wept when it was real: "Jesus wept" at Lazarus's tomb (John 11:35). He felt deeply what sin does to humanity. But he wasn't sitting there, constantly destroyed all the time. Yes, it broke his heart, and he was deeply acquainted with grief, but he carried on. He was still a strong man who was connected to his emotion.

When Jesus wept for Lazarus, he showed the perfect balance. He felt the grief deeply. He let others see his tears. Not for them, but because he actually felt them. But even through that, he still continued forward with his mission and purpose to raise Lazarus back to life and show that he had power over death. He could feel extremely deep emotions while being rooted in his identity and being grounded at the same time.

This is the difference between being subject to our emotions and observing them.

Sensitivity is not what we think of as walking into a room and knowing what everybody is feeling. I used to think that's what sensitivity was until I realized that's a trauma response. It's called hypervigilance. It means you've been trained your entire life, since you were a kid, that it was unsafe to express yourself without negative repercussions. So you either avoid your life and shut down any situation that could bring those emotions to the surface—which is how you protect yourself—or you gain hypervigilance, and you start to manipulate people without trying to. Usually both at the same time. It's not always intentional, but it can be subconscious.

Survival does not just involve food, water, and shelter. It also involves what we *perceive* as a threat—even if there isn't one. Then you get into the habit of creating something out of nothing, in the negative sense.

Walking into a room with hypervigilance was exhausting. I could feel what people were feeling without even having a conversation. I would walk into a bar in college and feel the confusion and anxiety of those around me, also projecting my own into the mess.

I would read someone's expressions or hear the tone of their voice, and it wouldn't match with what I sensed underneath. Nothing seemed or felt genuine. It was like everyone around me was untrustworthy, and I wanted to keep my distance.

Every social interaction became a chess match. I was three moves ahead, calculating responses, managing energies, trying to control outcomes before they happened. It wasn't connection—it was protection.

Ironically, I was wearing a mask, too, as I did this. I thought the environment had power over me instead of realizing that through Christ, I have power over the environment. Of course, I didn't know who Christ was then.

Hypervigilance allows us to notice what other people are feeling in a room, or what we think they're feeling, so that we can detect if they're a threat or not. So that sensitivity is actually stemming from trauma. But like God does with everything else, he can redeem it for good.

What the enemy meant for survival, God can transform for service. Amen.

From Curse to Gift

When I came to terms with understanding that hypervigilance was a trauma response, that allowed me to channel the gift not into trying to survive and just read people, but into being able to help people through their own journeys too.

In college, I realized I could deeply empathize with others. People would open up to me with things they wouldn't tell anyone else in the first conversation we had. Complete strangers would find themselves telling me their deepest fears, their hidden shames, their secret dreams. It was because I was projecting out an image of being someone who is put together, but behind closed doors, I was falling apart.

In the first retreat I led in 2024, when I took a group of entrepreneurs down to the jungles of El Salvador, I did one-on-ones with each of them. At least half of the group broke down in tears when I talked with them because it was like they were seen for the first time, after not seeing themselves most of their lives. This isn't from a place of ego but deep understanding. When you've mapped your own darkness, you can help others navigate theirs.

You need to first look at yourself objectively with your awareness. Then, through that awareness, you can accept what is actually there from a place of not being emotionally reactive to it. You have to be grounded in something bigger than yourself, or you'll get sucked into the tides. This is why you need to be anchored in God, the truth. Then you can sit in that space to help people heal themselves because you can sense what they feel more than they may in the moment. They may have no awareness of what's going on, but you may have complete awareness because you've learned how to use that situation as a gift.

The deeper you go into yourself, the deeper you can perceive into others.

This is a big part of where my depth of discernment has come from. I've been able to sense in people what is true or what is not because I've been able to look at myself and see *why* I'm able to sense other people—where the sensitivity comes from in the first place.

Because I can see the truth of it underneath the surface, I can see that truth now in other people. How can we see the truth in the world around us if we can't see it in ourselves? We're blind that way.

I had to learn how to love finding what the truth actually is.

You've got to take the plank out of your own eye before you're trying to take the speck out of your brother's, like Jesus talks about (Matt. 7:5). Otherwise, you're just projecting. And that doesn't actually heal anybody. That just becomes a coaching syndrome, and everyone around you unconsciously becomes your minion, which dehumanizes them.

This isn't actually loving because true leadership requires being a servant. And that first means serving the parts of yourself that have not been met, giving love to those areas of yourself, through God's definition and assistance. Patience, kindness, long suffering . . . all of these fruits that we give to others, have you ever given to yourself?

Yes, God is near to the brokenhearted, but what's up with this masochistic culture we live in? We need to stop being victims. God already said he will forgive us if we come to him, but we don't even receive it because we don't give the same to our own souls.

Bring light to those areas. Look deeply. Humble yourself so that you can chop off the pride that keeps you from seeing where you're blocking your own healing. You can't help others heal where you haven't.

The Feeling of Truth

Discernment is not a visual experience. It's something you feel, and it's subtle. You can just sense when something is off. You start to feel it in your soul, and your gut registers it. Your conscience picks up on right versus wrong. You can see it in the energy of people, how they're showing up and what they're saying.

Through that, you can start to know what's actually being said. I've been able to discern the truth in people just by looking in their eyes, hearing their voice, feeling their energy, and seeing how they shut down when they express something specific. I can see how they're trying to force a certain statement because I've seen all these things in myself.

I want you to remember that sensitivity is not a crime, and it's not a hindrance. It's a gift that you learn to balance with strength too. In fact, allowing yourself to be sensitive is a form of strength. Because a gift that is channeled into the right purpose and brought into balance with the other aspects of yourself—that's how you become whole and integrated. That's how you're actually able to help people.

It's not our job to force people to do anything. It's our job to be an embodiment of where we're trying to help them get to by just being ourselves. By being whole. That's what everybody's actually seeking—wholeness. We can and are called to model that through our relationship with Jesus.

The Codependency Trap

My most challenging experiences with taking on others' emotions have always been my romantic relationships.

I had to stop trying to soothe people's emotional experience, thinking that it was purely about me. When I did that, the woman in front of me wasn't able to fully feel safe enough to feel it without me trying to change what she was going through. Part of it was deeply caring to the point I'd overextend myself. Part of it was the fear of hurting her. Part of it was the fear of losing her.

The irony is that I recreated all three in each of those moments, which I can laugh at now. By trying to manage their emotions, I hurt them. By overextending myself, I lost myself. By fearing loss, I created distance.

I didn't realize that nobody is perfect and that we're all on our own journey, even together. Eventually, this led to a realization that I simply need to be a container and a rock grounded in loving truth.

But that wholeness, again, is only received through experiencing God's holiness. So we have to experience God's holiness for us to truly feel wholeness. That's why, above all, we have to seek God's will and what he's saying in the Bible and in prayer. We have to listen to that and see if our experience aligns with God's truth.

Reconnecting to Your Body

What I recommend is the next time you pray or meditate, just feel into your body and start making a connection with the areas you feel disconnected from. Because so many people live in their head today, they're thinking all the time. They're so disconnected from the body, and therefore, they're disconnected from the heart.

They don't know what to do because their gut connection is off—they're repressing it. Or they don't know how to love or experience love because they're not in their body and haven't been empathetic to themselves. They don't know how to connect to the heart.

So sit still for ten, twenty, or thirty minutes. The longer you can go, the better, but it's about quality and depth more than it is time. The purpose of this is to humble your body and break it under your authority, just like you'd break a wild horse. Allow whatever tension and frustration, anxiety, or twitchy feelings to come up in the area that is bringing them to the surface. Just connect to it and see what language is coming out of it without judging it.

Give all of it to Jesus, who is ready to take it from you.

Stop saying that it's good or bad. Just let it say what it is because every time you judge it, you're going to shut it down. And you can't uncover what the wound is underneath something if you're constantly trying to repress it. You just make it worse. It's going to gnaw at you and claw at you until you let it finally breathe.

So sit with it. Be with it. Once it expresses itself and you can see the root of it through that awareness, through that lack of emotional charge, once you've cleared it out, you can experience peace in that area through God's redemption.

I actually brought this issue to God about my prayer life and how it had been feeling dull. I was having a written conversation with him in my journal, and I said, "Now let's talk about prayer life. I feel it's been pretty bleh."

What he said was deeply insightful: "It has been weak. You have been performing for me instead of pouring into me. I want you to pour your pains, your pride, your fears, and your anger into me so I can wash it clean. I want to clean you out and ignite you. Next time you pray, just give it to me and expect me to return everything back to you clean like a washing machine. Just sit in my presence and let me wash you once you are done pouring."

It was a concept that was so simple, but so profound. He wanted to wash me clean.

Another thing I realized was that I was seeking an emotional experience, some crazy event to happen in prayer. The stillness and monotony are actually where our devotion grows stronger. It's not about the sensations, but they can happen if he decides that they do. The most important thing is to take them to God, and let him purify you.

The Art of Boundaries

Another important skill you need to learn is how to set boundaries. As you unlock your energetic and spiritual sensitivity, it can be easy to start to become emotionally or spiritually codependent on others. You attach yourself to them and take on their emotions as your own.

I had to start being conscious of making an "energetic wall" between myself and others before I would go into harder conversations. I was intentional about how my energy was connecting and made sure it stayed contained, while grounded in connection to God.

Imagine a wall between you and people whenever you are going deep emotionally. That's not a wall to block them off, but a floating energetic wall through which you can still connect, but they can't latch onto you or shake your inner stability, and you can't latch onto them. It creates healthy integrity between the two of you, where compassion can flow freely.

You're then able to be embodied in yourself while you notice what's going on, maintaining awareness of yourself and them. Through that boundary, then you will be able to lead the dynamic into harmony while also helping lead them out of darkness into light.

Here's the kicker, though . . . they have to want to meet you halfway.

A boundary is not about trying to control anyone around you. A boundary is being able to put up something inside of you that is energetically healthy but still allows you to relate to and interact with others. So you're still seeking connection, but it's a connection where you can both be healthy.

Opening to God's Love

When I actually allowed myself to open up to God with my full emotional experience, I felt seen, like I didn't have to push him away. I started trusting him and welcoming his love, both in a comforting and corrective form. It made me realize that he truly does want me and to see me. I felt like I could finally rest.

Regarding my lust struggles, I was alone for a time in the process. During that time frame, I poured out my heart to Jesus every single day. I would listen and sing worship music every night while breaking down in tears. It was a cathartic and healing time for me.

The deepest healing you can do is to allow yourself to be seen. Not the curated version. Not the performing version. Not the "good Christian" version. All of that is a show. Bring out the real, raw, messy, broken version of yourself that you're terrified anyone will reject. The real you.

It's simply a man or a woman relating with their Father at that point. No labels needed.

God doesn't want your performance. He wants your presence. He doesn't want your perfection. He wants your process. He can't heal what you won't reveal.

Finding the Balance

Unlock your energetic sensitivity, but also make sure it doesn't get the best of you. Once you find the balance of the two, it's going to make your journey to experiencing God's real discernment in a situation a lot better. And it's going to help you become an embodiment of what it means to experience God's healing.

Balance comes from being able to feel extremely deeply—such as having a hard conversation and empathizing, even shedding tears—but being rooted in your own identity and being grounded at the same time so you don't lose yourself in the emotional storm. Otherwise, you can't be an anchor of strength and love. Don't be afraid to unwind, but give the bulk of it to God. He is the only one who can take care of you with the deepest love.

Sensitivity without boundaries becomes codependency. Sensitivity without strength becomes fragility. Sensitivity without discernment becomes deception. But sensitivity submitted to God becomes a superpower.

You become someone who can enter the darkest rooms and not be overcome by the darkness. You can feel what others feel without drowning in it. You can see what others can't see without being destroyed by it. This is the gift hidden in what may have felt like a curse. This is the strength disguised as weakness. This is how God takes what the enemy meant for evil and uses it for good.

Your sensitivity was never the problem. The problem was believing you had to hide it from the One who gave it to you in the first place.

Chapter 7 Implementation: Week 8

Teaching Point

That sensitivity you've been taught to hide as weakness? It's actually your spiritual antenna—the very gift that lets you perceive the unseen realm. When you stop using it to protect yourself and start letting God use it to serve others, your wound transforms into your superpower.

Mindset Shift

From "Sensitivity makes me weak" to "Sensitivity helps me see beneath the surface."

Prayer

"Father, I confess I've believed the lie that sensitivity is weakness. I've hidden my emotions from you, thinking you'd punish me for having them and hardening my heart in the process. I've used trauma responses to protect myself instead of trusting you to protect me. Transform any hidden trauma into a gift for your glory. Help me feel deeply while staying rooted in you. Teach me to create healthy boundaries while staying open to love. I want to be seen by you—all of me, not just the parts I think are acceptable. Show me how to balance sensitivity with strength, just as Jesus did. In his name I pray, amen."

Scriptures to Meditate On

- "Jesus wept" (John 11:35 NIV).

- "In your anger do not sin: Do not let the sun go down while you are still angry" (Eph. 4:26 NIV).

- "Be strong and courageous. Do not be afraid; do not be discouraged, for the Lord your God will be with you wherever you go" (Josh. 1:9 NIV).

Action Steps

1. **Body scan practice.** Sit for twenty minutes in complete stillness. Scan your body from head to toe. Where do you feel tension? What emotions live there? Don't judge them—just notice. Let them speak. Take them to go. Journal what comes up without trying to fix it. Add ten minutes each day until you get to an hour.

2. **Boundary visualization.** Before your next difficult conversation, spend five minutes visualizing an energetic boundary. Picture a transparent wall that allows love to flow but keeps you from taking on others' emotions. Practice staying connected to your own body while engaging with theirs.

3. **Emotion integration.** Choose one "unacceptable" emotion you've hidden from God (anger, fear, lust, etcetera). Write him a letter being completely honest about it. Then sit in silence and let him respond. Notice: Does he reject you or draw closer? Document what you discover about his true nature.

CHAPTER 8 LIVING WITH EYES WIDE OPEN

Now it's time to integrate everything. You have the skill of discernment. You've learned to see. But how do you sustain it in a world that's constantly trying to blind you again?

The reality is that we live in a time when there are so many distractions. Everything wants to take your heart away from God. Everything wants to be worshiped. You have to maintain diligence, awareness, and fortitude in your heart so that you don't get sucked away.

This chapter isn't about just reading words. It's about practice. It's about taking everything you've learned and making it a living reality, not just head knowledge.

Digestion without application is just information, not transformation.

Your Sanctuary Strategy

One of the most powerful things you can do is spend time in nature. Not as an escape, but as a reset. Not as a vacation, but as a vision quest.

At least once a quarter—mark it in your calendar right now—get away. Get a cabin. Find an Airbnb somewhere remote. Go camping if that's all you can afford. The point is to completely separate from your normal environment. If you can't afford to do it, you can't afford not to.

Here's what happens when you do this: Your nervous system completely relaxes. You gain more energy naturally from within. You become more loving, less agitated and frustrated, less caught in comparison with others, more connected to your heart. You'll be shocked at how much more you can discern God's voice and promptings when you remove yourself from worldly distractions.

But here's the key—when you go, you're not going to *do* something. You're going to *be* with Someone. The hardest part is always remembering that you are rooted in him by who you are to him, not just what you do for him. Make sure to get off of your phone when there!

Action Step 1: Schedule Your Quarterly Retreat

- Open your calendar right now.
- Block out two to three days every quarter for the next year.
- Make it nonnegotiable.
- Tell everyone in advance you'll be unreachable.
- Choose places in nature where you can walk, hike, or simply sit.

If you can't get away for a few days, start with a full day once a month. If you can't do that, commit to four hours every Sunday. No excuses. Your spiritual sight depends on it.

The Stillness Protocol

You need to continue being diligent and disciplined in your meditation and awareness exercises. Why? Because they help you see the separation between your emotions and when God is speaking to you in that still, small voice, telling you the truth.

In that moment of awareness, when an event happens, there's a tiny amount of time between emotional reaction and taking action. In that space, you decide if you're going to let the emotion rule you or if you're going to rule the emotion. Awareness brings power through the ability to choose so you are no longer a slave to the unconscious.

This timing—that little space—can only be captured if you spend more time cultivating your awareness and being in stillness in the presence of God. That's going to help you have more self-control.

Action Step 2: Daily Stillness Practice

- Set a timer for twenty minutes every morning.
- Sit in complete silence.
- When emotions arise, don't react or suppress.
- Ask: "What is this emotion telling me?"
- Let it speak without judgment.
- Notice the gap between feeling and action.
- Choose your response from that place of awareness.

Remember: Don't force emotions to come up. You'll make them hide or reinforce them. Let them arise naturally. Treat them like a little kid inside you that needs your love and presence. As the emotion clears out, what's left over is the experiential wisdom and truth that we talked about earlier in this book.

The Detox Blueprint

Your body affects your spirit. When your central nervous system is jacked up all the time, you won't hear God clearly. It causes inflammation, stress in the body. Your emotions get out of whack. Life feels disconnected and ungrounded. It leads to anxiety and lack of mental clarity, and makes it hard to discern what voice is talking to you.

Action Step 3: The Thirty-Day Reset

Weeks 1 to 2: Caffeine Detox

- Gradually reduce caffeine over fourteen days, being fully off by day seven and going cold turkey the rest.
- Switch to herbal tea or water. Use nootropics to mitigate withdrawal if needed.
- Notice: How does your energy change?
- Document: When do you actually feel tired versus artificially wired?
- Observe: How does this affect your prayer life?

If you need additional resources, check out my holistic wellness brand, the Stampede Network, at thestampedenetwork.com.

Weeks 3 to 4: Tech Fasting

- Choose one day per week for complete phone and computer fast.
- Start with eight hours if a full day seems impossible.
- Put your phone in another room at night.
- Stay off screens for the first hour after waking.

- Stay off screens for the last hour before bed.

What you'll discover: The Spirit, when we allow it to take over and heal us, provides an abundant source of energy already within us. We've been led to believe that things like caffeine alone energizes us, when in reality, we end up crashing. God is the life and energy Source you're actually seeking, with way more clarity and peace.

The Separation Solution

Too many voices in your head will take you away from the Voice that actually matters. We do want community, but we also need solitude to hear him clearly. We can start to confuse other people for him if we don't have that time.

Action Step 4: Strategic Solitude

- Fast from social relationships periodically (this is biblical).
- Take one evening per week with no social plans.
- Spend that time in prayer and Bible reading.
- Notice what thoughts you've been running from.
- Learn to enjoy stillness.
- Practice being alone without being lonely.

If solitude is hard for you, there's probably a relationship with your thoughts you're running from. This is your opportunity to face it.

Reading the Room Versus Reading the Spirit

You've learned about emotional hypervigilance—how trauma taught you to read every room for threats. Now it's time to transform that curse into controlled blessing.

Action Step 5: Boundary Building Exercise

Before entering any emotionally charged situation:

- Spend five minutes in prayer.
- Visualize an energetic boundary around you.
- Set an intention: "I will feel *with* them, not *as* them."
- Practice staying rooted in your own body.
- After the interaction, check: Did I take on their emotions?
- If yes, spend ten minutes releasing what isn't yours.

This isn't about becoming cold or distant. It's about being a lighthouse—firmly planted while still shining light for those lost at sea.

The Word as Your Foundation

Here's what you need to understand: The Bible isn't just a book to read. It's a mirror that shows you who you really are and who God really is.

Spend time in the Word every single day. Not out of guilt. Not out of obligation. But from the bottom of your heart, knowing it will save your life.

Don't worship the words. Worship the Word.

There's a big difference. Don't get stuck in worshiping the words being said. Instead, feel into the essence behind them. Let the Bible read you instead of just you reading it.

Action Step 6: The Bible Immersion Method

- Choose one book of the Bible.
- Read the same chapter every day for a week.

- Each day, ask: "What is God showing me about myself?"
- Write down what convicts you.
- Most importantly: Apply one thing immediately.
- Don't move to the next chapter until you've applied something.

God can make you aware of something, but you have to choose to surrender to change. You have to be willing to see where you've been out of alignment and consciously choose to put it into practice like Jesus says: "Why do you call me 'Lord, Lord,' and do not do what I say?" (Luke 6:46 NIV).

Becoming a Walking Temple

It is your job to walk around as a living temple of vision, being guided by God. As you walk in the image of God as a son or daughter, you naturally become a light to others. By being a light, you can see further than the darkness and shine the way for others trying to find their way home.

You become the lighthouse while they may be a boat that's stuck or lost at sea. Through your discernment, you'll be able to see the blind spots in yourself and others that most miss.

Action Step 7: The Lighthouse Practice

- Each morning, declare: "I am a carrier of God's light today."
- Ask God: "Who needs to see your light through me? Guide me to be a light today."
- Stay sensitive to promptings throughout the day.
- When someone shares a struggle, ask yourself:
  - "What truth have I learned through similar pain?"
  - "How can I share hope without minimizing their experience?"

- Remember: You can only guide others through territory you've walked.

We only know the truth of a situation when we've gone through it ourselves. We can know about something, but truly knowing requires walking it out.

The Rereading Revolution

Read this book multiple times. Why? Because you're going to go through different seasons of life, and all seasons are controlled by God. As you go through those seasons, you'll have more awareness, more perspectives to view from. You'll see things differently.

Something may pop out in a different season that didn't fully resonate in this one. As your eyes continue to develop, this book will make more and more sense.

Action Step 8: The Seasonal Review

- Put blatant reminders in your calendar for six months and one year from now to read again.
- When you reread, ask:
  - "What do I see now that I couldn't see before?"
  - "What struggles from before have become wisdom?"
  - "Where am I still blind?"
- Document your growth.
- Share your testimony with someone who needs hope.

Discernment isn't about always going out and finding more. It's about looking deeper at what's already in front of you.

The Integration Checklist

Here's your practical road map for the next ninety days:

Days 1 through 30: Foundation

- ☐ Establish daily twenty-minute stillness practice
- ☐ Begin caffeine detox
- ☐ Schedule first quarterly retreat
- ☐ Start Bible immersion with one book
- ☐ Practice emotional awareness gaps daily

Days 31 through 60: Deepening

- ☐ Add weekly tech fasting day
- ☐ Implement boundary visualization before difficult conversations
- ☐ Begin weekly solitude evenings
- ☐ Journal your spiritual sight improvements
- ☐ Share one testimony of transformation

Days 61 through 90: Expansion

- ☐ Take your first extended nature retreat
- ☐ Help someone else begin their journey to see
- ☐ Reread chapters that challenged you most
- ☐ Evaluate what has become natural versus what needs work
- ☐ Plan your next season of growth

The Ultimate Goal

If I could sum up this entire book for you, it would be this: Don't just try to seek discernment. Don't just try to seek vision. Seek the One who gives you all those things. Seek the One who is love in totality and who can make you whole.

Through that, you will come into a relationship with your Creator, and it will start to light you up from the inside out. When you become the embodiment of what God's love is—when you truly and deeply know it inside yourself—fear will have no place inside or outside you anymore.

Light always casts out darkness. God's love always casts out fear.

If you are the embodiment of God's love and know it, fear has no place around you. This is when you will truly be walking in your purpose.

The journey from blindness to sight isn't a onetime event. It's a daily choice. Every morning, you wake up in a world trying to muddy your telescope again. But now you have the tools and the knowledge, and most importantly, now you have the relationship with the One who is sight itself.

Stop trying to see. Start seeking the One who sees all. In finding him, you'll find everything else you've been looking for—including yourself.

Chapter 8 Implementation: First Steps

Teaching Point

Everything crystallizes here: Maintaining true spiritual sight and identity isn't about perfect practices but about choosing relationship over religiosity every single day. The transformation happens when you stop trying to see for yourself and start living in union with the One who *is* sight.

Mindset Shift

From "I must strive to maintain vision" to "I must stay connected and in alignment with God to see, while letting him guide me through his grace."

Prayer

"Father, I commit to living with eyes wide open. Give me the discipline to maintain these practices when life gets busy. Give me deeper fear of the Lord so that I value being in your presence over simply receiving presents. Help me create space for you in nature, in stillness, in your Word. Transform my awareness into action. Make me a lighthouse for others who are lost in the darkness I once knew. I choose to seek you above all else, knowing that in finding you, I find everything. Keep my spiritual sight clear in this chaotic world. In Jesus's name, amen."

Scriptures to Meditate On

- "Be still, and know that I am God" (Ps. 46:10 ESV).
- "Your word is a lamp for my feet and a light to my path" (Ps. 119:105 ESV).

- "You are the light of the world. A city that is set on a hill cannot be hidden" (Matt. 5:14 NKJV).

Action Steps

1. **Right now.** Open your calendar and schedule your first quarterly retreat. Make it non-negotiable.
2. **Tomorrow morning.** Begin your twenty-minute stillness practice. Set your alarm twenty minutes earlier if needed.
3. **This week.** Choose which book of the Bible to immerse yourself in for the next thirty days. Start with John if you're unsure.

Thank you for trusting me to bring you on this journey. Make sure to keep focusing on putting this knowledge into action so that true transformation becomes a way of being in your life!

—Mason Kuhr

Read the next page for continued action steps.

HERE'S WHAT TO DO NEXT

Remember, this is more than just ingesting knowledge. It's about repentance and lasting transformation.

Whenever you're ready, here are four ways I can help you take the next step on your journey:

1. Access To My God-Led Leadership Community

By reading this book and saying yes to yourself, you know what to do. Now it's time to walk it out with others seeking God like you.

Visit https://whop.com/lionheart/ to get access to a ninety-day leadership transformation program and holistic reset protocol.

2. Get Your Free Self-Mastery Kit & More from the Stampede Network

If you need additional tools to help with your transformation, go to https://hoo.be/mase as well as thestampedenetwork.com to get your free bonuses.

3. Hire Mason to Speak

If you are looking for deep transformation at your conference, event, church, or mastermind, let's talk!

Email seetheunseenbook@gmail.com with "SPEAKING" in the subject line. You can also go to masonkuhr.com

4. Connect on Social Media

Let's keep the transformation going! This is just the start. I'd love to connect with you on all social platforms and hear your testimony. You can find me on all socials at @masonkuhr. Also check out my worship house music by House of Purpose everywhere.

ACKNOWLEDGMENTS

I want to thank everyone who has been part of the journey, from my parents and family, to friends, romantic relationships, business partners both past and present.

Thank you for reflecting back to me the parts of myself where I was still seeking wholeness, and showing me areas of myself I needed to return to God.

Relationships are the whole point of why we're here, and there are too many to count, yet all of them have played an integral role of introducing me to myself so that I may eventually come to know who God is.

Above all, I want to thank Jesus. The whole reason I wrote this book was for it to be a testimony to his transformative power.

Thank you for setting up my life in such a way that it would lead me back to you, and give me meaning, identity, and purpose in the process.

ABOUT THE AUTHOR

Mason Kuhr is a builder, creator, and spiritual guide whose life has been shaped by a relentless pursuit of truth. From years as an athlete to climbing mountains across the world, from launching a multimillion-dollar holistic wellness brand to leading people back to God through inner healing—Mason's path has been anything but conventional.

What began as a journey through biohacking, health, creation, adventure, and entrepreneurship evolved into something deeper: a call to help people return to the presence of God, align their identity with truth, and rebuild their lives from the inside out so they can fully step into their God-given purpose. Mason has led hundreds of thousands through detoxing the body, rewiring the mind, healing emotional patterns, and reconnecting with God at a deeper level.

Today he speaks, writes, hosts retreats, creates music, and mentors leaders with a rare blend of honesty, spiritual discernment, grounded masculinity, and rooted clarity. His mission is simple:

embody the spiritual-warrior within, restore the heart, and lead God's children back home into true relationship.

He lives this message—not as a perfect man, but as a man committed to walking with God in the tension, the questions, and the continual unfolding of truth.

See the Unseen is not just his book.

It is his life lived out loud and captured in these pages.

Some of his current initiatives are the Stampede Network, focused on inner transformation by using God's natural medicine; the Lionheart Project, a ministry for faith-first leadership development; and projects such as House of Purpose, which is a new spin on worship music.

Catch him on all platforms @masonkuhr.